The Myth of Digital Democracy

The Myth of Digital Democracy

Matthew Hindman

PRINCETON UNIVERSITY PRESS *Princeton and Oxford*

Copyright © 2009 by Princeton University Press

Published by Princeton University Press, 41 William Street, Princeton,
New Jersey 08540

In the United Kingdom: Princeton University Press, 6 Oxford Street, Woodstock,
Oxfordshire OX20 1TW

Library of Congress Cataloging-in-Publication Data

Hindman, Matthew Scott, 1976–
    The myth of digital democracy / Matthew Hindman.
        p. cm.
    Includes bibliographical references.
    ISBN 978-0-691-13761-2 (hardcover : alk. paper) — ISBN 978-0-691-13868-8
(pbk. : alk. paper)   1. Political participation—United States.   2. Internet in political
campaigns—United States.   3. Internet—Political aspects—United States.   I. Title.
    JK1764.H56 2009
    320.9730285'4678—dc22   2008005147

British Library Cataloging-in-Publication Data is available

This book has been composed in Times Roman

Printed on acid-free paper. ∞

press.princeton.edu

Printed in the United States of America

10 9 8 7 6 5 4 3 2

For Chuck, Karen, and Nathan

Contents

Illustrations

Acknowledgments

This book has been the work of many years, and the list of debts I have incurred in writing it is long. The earliest parts of *The Myth of Digital Democracy* began with my doctoral dissertation at Princeton University, supervised by Larry Bartels, Jennifer Hochshild, and Paul DiMaggio. This book would not exist without their stewardship of that thesis project and willingness to let me begin an untraditional line of research. Markus Prior, who later joined the project as the fourth reader, also provided many insights and critiques. My peers at Princeton were a continual source of helpful comments, and I am especially grateful to Chris Karpowitz, Rob Rodgers, Chris Mackie, Jonathan Ladd, and Gabriel Lenz.

Early work on this project benefited greatly from two years as a fellow at Harvard University, during which I was affiliated with both the Department of Government in the Graduate School of Arts and Sciences, and the National Center for Digital Government in the John F. Kennedy School of Government. While many in the government department and the visiting fellows program offered helpful advice, Daniel Ho, Francesca Gino, James Fowler, Kosuke Imai, and Alison Post deserve special thanks.

The National Center for Digital Government (NCDG) provided me with fellowship funding for my final year of graduate school, through National Science Foundation grant number 0131923. In directing the NCDG, Jane Fountain and David Lazer fostered a fertile academic environment, and both offered wise counsel. NCDG fellows Audrey

Selian, Rajiv Shah, Maria Binz-Scharf, Ines Mergel, and Kenneth Neil Cukier helped refine this research too. Kenn's contributions to the project as my office mate, editor, and sounding board were especially substantial.

Unusually for a political science project, this book depended at several junctures on corporate support. I am grateful to NEC Research Labs in Princeton, New Jersey, for lending its staff, software, and hardware, and to Gary Flake for setting up that arrangement. NEC researchers Kostas Tsioutsiouliklis and Judy A. Johnson, my collaborators on the Googlearchy research, were a pleasure to work with. The research presented here in chapter 3 would have been impossible without their expertise.

Hitwise Competitive Intelligence generously provided access to their treasure trove of Web usage data. Heather Hopkins, Bill Tancer, and the Hitwise support staff have my heartfelt thanks.

Other contributions also deserve recognition. Lada Adamic, at the time a member of Hewlett-Packard's Web research group, supplied both data and helpful advice. The GUESS visualization software created by Eytan Adar, another member of the Hewlett-Packard Web research group, was used to create the Web maps in chapter 4. Yuri Rapoport of Seaglex Software provided tools to help collect and analyze search engine results. Paul Jungwirth and Nathan Hindman helped me find and fix bugs in my own software code.

An earlier version of chapter 2 was published in the March 2005 issue of *Perspectives on Politics*.[1] James McCann, Alan Abramowitz, the three anonymous reviewers, and the editorial staff of *Perspectives* all contributed to that portion of the book.

I am grateful to my colleagues at Arizona State University for their insights and support. Kim Fridkin, Pat Kenney, Colin Elman, Paul Goren, David Guston, Rudy Espino, and Merlyna Lim all offered important guidance. Several research assistants contributed to the book as well. Carol Lynn Bower and Risto Karinen provided help in coding user search queries, and Roland Maldonado helped conduct the blogger census. Anthony Hayes, an undergraduate honors student, was a particularly providential addition to the project. His smart and tireless work to map Web traffic went far beyond the call of duty.

---

[1] "The Real Lessons of Howard Dean: Reflections on the First Digital Campaign," *Perspectives on Politics* 3 (1): 121–28.

In addition to all of those named above, I have been privileged to discuss portions of this work in many settings over many years with many smart people. While any listing of this group is sure to be incomplete, it does include (in no particular order) Eszter Hargittai, Bruce Bimber, Helen Nissenbaum, Bernardo Huberman, Albert-László Barabási, Paul Starr, Clay Shirky, Yochai Benkler, Eli Noam, Lance Bennett, Robert Pepper, Daniel Drezner, Paul Herrnson, Helen Margetts, Ralph Schroeder, Diana Owen, Joe Turow, Arthur Lupia, Gisella Sin, Ben Edelman, Richard Davis, and Cynthia Rudin. While not everyone in this group has shared my conclusions, each has shared insights that I have tried to incorporate into the text.

Lastly, I would like to thank my friends and family. The research presented here has spanned many transitions in my personal and professional life, and I am grateful beyond words for their unfailing love and support.

The Myth of Digital Democracy

One

The Internet and the "Democratization" of Politics

The world has arrived at an age of cheap complex devices of
great reliability; and something is bound to come of it.
—Vannevar Bush, "As We May Think," July 1945

In March 1993, a group of college students at the University of Illinois
posted a small piece of software onto the Internet. The program was called
Mosaic, and it was the world's first graphical Web browser. Prior to Mosaic, the World Wide Web, invented a few years previously by an English
physicist working in Geneva, was but one of a number of applications that
ran on top of the Internet. Mosaic changed everything.[1] Unlike the cum-
bersome text-based programs that had preceded it, Mosaic made the Web a
colorful and inviting medium that anyone could navigate. The Internet was
soon transformed from a haven for techies and academics into the fastest-
growing communications technology in history.

The release of Mosaic was the starting gun for the Internet revolution.
Mosaic was quickly commercialized as the Netscape browser, and Netscape's public stock offering in 1995 ushered in the Internet stock market
bubble. But almost from the moment that it became a mass medium, the
Internet was seen as more than just a way to revamp commerce and the
practice of business. Its most important promise, many loudly declared,
was political. New sources of online information would make citizens more
informed about politics. New forms of Internet organizing would help
recruit previously inactive citizens into political participation. Cyberspace

[1] For two good studies of the early history of the Internet, see Abbatte 1998; Hafner 1998. For
a firsthand account of the creation of the Web, see Berners-Lee 2000.

would become a robust forum for political debate. The openness of the Internet would allow citizens to compete with journalists for the creation and dissemination of political information.

A decade and a half after Mosaic transformed the Internet, many contend that at least part of the Internet's political promise has been fulfilled. Those arguing that the Internet is transforming politics come from the upper echelons of politics, journalism, public policy, and law. Howard Dean campaign manager Joe Trippi effuses that "the Internet is the most democratizing innovation we've ever seen, more so even than the printing press" (2005, 235). The Internet's increasing importance may be the only thing that Trippi and Bush-Cheney campaign manager Ken Mehlman agree on. The key lesson of the 2004 campaign, according to Mehlman, is that "technology has broken the monopoly of the three [television] networks," and "instead of having one place where everyone gets information, there are thousands of places" (quoted in Crowe 2005).

Other prominent public officials have concluded that the Internet's influence extends beyond the campaign trail. Former Senate majority leader Trent Lott, who resigned after a few bloggers highlighted racially charged remarks, acknowledged the Internet's power, grumbling that "bloggers claim I was their first pelt, and I believe that. I'll never read a blog" (quoted in Chaddock 2005). Federal Communications Commission chair Michael Powell used the Internet to justify looser regulation of broadcast media, explaining that "information technology...has a democratizing effect.... With a low cost computer and an Internet connection every one has a chance to 'get the skinny,' the 'real deal,' to see the wizard behind the curtain" (2002).

Journalists, too, have concluded that the Internet's challenge to traditional media is real, and that the medium "will give new voice to people who've felt voiceless" (Gillmor 2004, xviii). Radio host and Emmy-winning former news anchor Hugh Hewitt (a blogger himself) writes that "the power of elites to determine what [is] news via a tightly controlled dissemination system [has been] shattered. The ability and authority to distribute text are now truly democratized" (2005, 70–71). Former NBC News and PBS president Lawrence Grossman concludes that the Internet gives citizens "a degree of empowerment they never had before" (1995, 146). CNN president Jonathan Klein has taken such claims even further, famously worrying that the Internet has given too much power to "a guy sitting in his living room in his pajamas" (quoted in Colford 2004). Tom Brokaw has argued that bloggers represent "a democratization of news" (quoted in Guthrie 2004). Brian Williams, who succeeded Brokaw as anchor, complained that he had spent "all of my life, developing credentials to cover my field of work, and now I'm up against a guy named Vinny in an efficiency apartment in the Bronx who hasn't left the efficiency apartment in two years" (quoted in O'Gorman 2007). *New York Times* reporter Judith Miller laid part of the blame for her travails on overzealous bloggers, claiming that *Times* editor in chief Bill Keller told her, "You are radioactive. . . . You can see it in the blogs" (quoted in Shafer 2006). Bloggers also played a role in the resignation of Howell Raines, the *Times'* previous editor in chief, in the aftermath of the Jayson Blair scandal (Kahn and Kellner 2004).

The notion that the Internet is making public discourse more accessible has even found expression in case law. In striking down the Communications Decency Act, the U.S. Supreme Court emphasized the potential of the Internet to create a radically more diverse public sphere:

> Any person or organization with a computer connected to the Internet can "publish" information. . . .
>
> Through the use of chat rooms, any person with a phone line can become a town crier with a voice that resonates farther than it could from any soapbox. Through the use of Web pages, mail exploders, and newsgroups, the same individual can become a pamphleteer. As the District Court found, "the content on the Internet is as diverse as human thought."[2]

Given the high court's decision, it is perhaps unsurprising that in *John Doe No. 1 v. Cahill* (2005), the Delaware Supreme Court held as a matter of fact that "the Internet is a unique democratizing medium" that allows "more and diverse people to engage in public debate."[3]

It may be comforting to believe that the Internet is making U.S. politics more democratic. In a few important ways, though, beliefs that the Internet is democratizing politics are simply wrong.

---

[2] *Reno v. ACLU*, U.S. 521 (1997).

[3] *John Doe No. 1 v. Cahill et al.*, DE 266, sec. III-A (2005).

Democratization and Political Voice

This book is about the Internet's impact on U.S. politics. It deals with some of the central questions in this debate: Is the Internet making politics less exclusive? Is it empowering ordinary citizens at the expense of elites? Is it, as we are often told, "democratizing" U.S. politics?

On the one hand, those arguing for the political importance of the Internet seem to have been vindicated by recent events. Online political organizations, such as the left-leaning group MoveOn.org, have attracted millions of members, raised tens of millions of dollars, and become a key force in electoral politics.[4] Even more important, the 2004 and 2008 election cycles showed that candidates themselves can use the Internet to great effect. This book looks closely at how Dean used the Internet to re-cruit tens of thousands of previously inactive citizens as campaign vol-unteers. Dean's success at raising money from small, online donations— along with the subsequent successes of Wesley Clark, John Kerry, and even George W. Bush—challenged almost everything political scientists thought they knew about political giving. Barack Obama's primary cam-paign has emphasized the same lessons. And increasingly, the Web seems to have empowered a huge corps of individuals who function both as citizen-journalists and political commentators. Collectively, the weekly readership of the top dozen political blogs rivals that of *Time*, *Newsweek*, or the *New York Times*.[5]

But if the successes of Internet politics are increasingly obvious, they have also tempted us to draw the wrong conclusions. If we want to un-derstand the fate of politics in the Internet age, we also need to acknowl-edge new and different types of exclusivity that shape online politics. In a host of areas, from political news to blogging to issue advocacy, this book shows that online speech follows winners-take-all patterns. Paradoxically, the extreme "openness" of the Internet has fueled the creation of new political elites. The Internet's successes at democratizing politics are real. Yet the medium's failures in this regard are less acknowledged and ulti-mately just as profound.

---

[4] For a scholarly discussion of MoveOn, see Kahn and Kellner 2004; Chadwick 2006.

[5] This conclusion comes from comparing circulation figures from the Audit Bureau of Cir-culation (online at AccessABC.org) with blog visitor data from SiteMeter.com compiled by N. Z. Bear (2004).

The argument of this book has several parts, and I expect a few of the claims I make to be controversial. Part of the problem with debates about Internet politics, however, comes from the vocabulary that is used. Because the language is fuzzy, much of the reasoning has been, too. So the first task of this book is to define what, exactly, we are talking about.

Defining "Democratization"

At the heart of this semantic problem are conflicting definitions and claims about the word democracy itself. Those who discuss the Internet's impact on political life are enormously fond of the word democratization, yet public discussion has used the word democratize in at least two distinct senses. If the two are confused, the argument I offer here will make little sense.

One meaning of the word democratize is normative. As George Orwell wrote in "Politics and the English Language," "The word Fascism has now no meaning except in so far as it signifies 'something not desirable' " (1946). Orwell also noted that the word democracy had been "similarly abused. . . . It is almost universally felt that when we call a country democratic we are praising it: consequently the defenders of every kind of regime claim that it is a democracy, and fear that they might have to stop using that word if it were tied down to any one meaning."

The discussion of Internet politics has been mired in this same problem. To say that the Internet is a democratic technology is to imply that the Internet is a good thing. This problem is not new: previous communications technologies, from the telegraph to the rotary press to radio and television, were similarly proclaimed to be democratic (see, for example, Bimber 2003a; Starr 2004; Barnouw 1966; McChesney 1990). Nonetheless, popular enthusiasm for technology has made a sober appraisal of the Internet's complicated political effects more difficult. Discussions of technical matters easily morph into unhelpful referenda on the technology's social value.

Broad claims about the goodness of the Internet are, of course, hard to refute. The Internet now touches countless areas of economic, social, and political life. Adding up and evaluating every impact of this technology is beyond the scope of this book. This volume tries to avoid such overarching judgments about the value of the technology.

The central argument therefore focuses on the second definition of democratization. This definition is descriptive. Most talk about Internet-fueled democratization has been quite specific about the political changes that the Internet ostensibly promotes. In these accounts, the Internet is re-distributing political influence; it is broadening the public sphere, increasing political participation, involving citizens in political activities that were previously closed to them, and challenging the monopoly of traditional elites. This second definition of democratization presumes first and foremost that the technology will amplify the political voice of ordinary citizens.

This book is a work of political science, and political voice has long been a central concern of the discipline. As Sidney Verba, Kay Lehman Schlozman, and Henry E. Brady declare in *Voice and Equality*, "meaningful democratic participation requires that the voices of citizens in politics be clear, loud, and equal" (1995, 509). In this regard, political scientists have naturally been interested in the sorts of activities discussed in a typical high school civics course. We want to know not just which citizens vote but also which are most likely to write a letter to their senator, what sorts of citizens volunteer for political campaigns, and what types of individuals give money to political interest groups. Political scientists have long known that patterns of political participation favor traditionally advantaged groups—though the magnitude of this disparity varies greatly across different avenues of participation.[6]

In recent years, some have suggested that the Internet makes it necessary to expand the study of political voice to include online activities and online speech. Most studies of political voice were written when few Americans were online. Partly, political scientists have wanted to know about online analogues of traditional political acts. If sending a letter to one's congressperson deserves to be studied as part of political voice, surely sending an e-mail does too; if mailing a check to a candidate counts, so does an online credit card donation.[7]

If political scientists have mostly talked about voice in the context of political participation, others have wondered whether the Internet might force us to reconsider more fundamental assumptions. Many areas of political science, such as scholarship on public opinion, have drawn a sharp distinction between the political elites (including journalists) who craft and

---

[6] On this point, see Schattschneider 1960; Verba, Schlozman, and Brady 1995; Rosenstone and Hansen 1993; Lijphart 1997.

[7] Of course, elected representatives themselves may not consider an e-mail to be equivalent to a handwritten letter; for a discussion of the relative weight that members of Congress attach to constituent correspondence, see Lebert 2003; Frantzich 2004.

disseminate media messages, and the mass public that receives them (see, for example, Zaller 1992, Page and Shapiro 1992). Yet some have claimed that the Internet has blurred these traditionally ironclad distinctions. As Arthur Lupia and Gisella Sin put it,

> The World Wide Web... allows individuals—even children—to post, at minimal cost, messages and images that can be viewed instantly by global audiences. It is worth remembering that as recently as the early 1990s, such actions were impossible for all but a few world leaders, public figures, and entertainment companies—and even for them only at select moments. Now many people take such abilities for granted. (2003, 316)

If citizens could write their own news, create their own political commentary, and post their views before a worldwide audience, this would surely have profound implications for political voice. Scholars such as Michael Schudson (1999) have talked about "monitorial citizenship," suggesting that democracy can work tolerably well even if citizens only pay attention to politics when things go obviously wrong. In this account, just responding effectively to "fire alarms" or "burglar alarms" can give citizens a strong political voice (Zaller 2003; Prior 2006; but see Bennett 2003a). From this perspective, the Internet might make monitoring more effective. It might allow citizens themselves to play part of the role traditionally reserved for the organized press.

Political philosophers have also worked in recent years to expand the notion of political voice, with a torrent of scholarship on what has come to be called deliberative democracy. Much of the initial credit for refocusing scholarly attention goes to Jürgen Habermas (1981, 1996); yet what John Dryzek (2002) terms the "deliberative turn" in political thought now includes numerous prominent scholars (Rawls 1995; Cohen 1989; Nino 1998; Gutmann and Thompson 1996; Ackerman and Fishkin 2004). Despite their differences, these deliberative democrats all agree that democracy should be more than just a process for bargaining and the aggregation of preferences. All suggest that true participation requires citizens to engage in direct discussion with other citizens. The Internet's political impacts have often been viewed through the lens that deliberative democrats have provided. The hope has been that the Internet would expand the public sphere, broadening both the range of ideas discussed and the number of citizens allowed to participate.

Scholars thus disagree about what precisely citizenship requires and what our definitions of political voice should therefore include. Yet proponents of participatory citizenship, deliberative citizenship, and monitorial citizenship all focus on political equality—and particularly on making formal political equality meaningful in practice. This book concentrates on areas where the overlap among these concerns is likely to be the greatest and where the Internet's political impact has been the clearest. It examines the Dean campaign, online political advocacy communities, and the rise of blogs. It looks at the role of search engines in guiding citizens to political content and attempts to measure where exactly citizens go when they visit online political Web sites. In each case, this book searches for evidence that the Internet has expanded the voice of ordinary citizens.

Framed in this way, broad questions about democratization can be broken down into a series of smaller, and ultimately answerable, questions. Some of these deal with political voice as traditionally conceived: Are there types of political participation that have been increased by the Internet? Have significant numbers of previously inactive citizens been recruited into political activism? Other questions deal with claims that the Internet will challenge vested political interests, encourage public debate, or even blur traditional distinctions between elites and the mass public. Exactly how open is the architecture of the Internet? Are online audiences more decentralized than audiences in traditional media? How many citizens end up getting heard in cyberspace? Are those who *do* end up getting heard a more accurate reflection of the broader public?

The main task of this book is to provide answers to this series of questions. I also attempt, more cautiously, to say how these small answers together paint a broader picture of Internet politics. Yet in order to understand this larger project, several points must be made first. Chief among them is to explain how the critique of online politics I put forward differs from the visions of the Internet that other scholars have offered.

A Different Critique

Scholars of the Internet have generally been more cautious than public figures and journalists, but they too have focused on claims that the Internet is democratizing politics. Researchers have come at this issue from a variety of perspectives—and partly as a result, we now have a more complete picture of the Internet than we did a decade ago. At the same time, scholars have also come to conflicting conclusions about the Internet's political impacts.

One long-standing reason for skepticism has been the so-called digital divide. Even as Internet use expanded dramatically during the 1990s, disadvantaged groups—blacks, Hispanics, the poor, the elderly, the undereducated, and those in rural areas—continued to lag behind in their access to and use of the Net (NTIA 2000, 2002; Bimber 2000; Wilhelm 2000). While more recent data show that some gaps have narrowed, important differences remain, particularly with respect to age, race, and education (Dijk 2005; Warschauer 2004; Mossberger, Tolbert, and Stansbury 2003). Increasingly, research has shown that the skills needed to use the Web effectively are perhaps even more stratified than access itself (Hargittai 2003; Dijk 2005; DiMaggio et al. 2004; Norris 2001). Recent surveys indicate, too, that growth in the online population has slowed dramatically since 2001, dampening expectations that a rising Internet tide would quickly end such inequalities (Bimber 2003b).

Aside from the digital divide, scholars have suggested other reasons that the Internet may have little impact on politics—or even change politics for the worse. Some have proposed that the movement of traditional actors and political interests online means that cyberpolitics will mirror traditional patterns—that, as Michael Margolis and David Resnick put it, online politics is simply "politics as usual" (2000; see also Davis 1998). Others have worried that market concentration within Internet-related technology sectors—from network hardware to Internet service providers—would compromise the medium's openness (see, for example, Noam 2003). The search engine marketplace has been a particular locus of concern; as Lucas Introna and Helen Nissenbaum explain, search engines "provide essential access to the Web both to those with something to say and offer as well as those wishing to hear and find" (2000, 181).

Others have worried that instead of too much concentration, the Internet will provide too little. Cass Sunstein contends that the Internet may mean the end of broadcasting; with audiences widely dispersed over millions of Web sites, general-interest intermediaries will disappear, political polarization will accelerate, and public debate will coarsen (2001; see also Shapiro 1999; Wilhelm 2000). Robert Putnam is likewise concerned that the Internet will produce "cyberapartheid" and "cyberbalkanization" (2000). Joseph Nye even suggests that "the demise of broadcasting and the rise of narrowcasting may fragment the sense of community and legitimacy that underpins central governments" (Karmark and Nye 2002, 10).

Against this backdrop, we have seen an explosion of scholarship documenting Internet-organized political activism that looks strikingly different from traditional patterns. From established interest groups such as Environmental Defense to brand-new organizations like MoveOn, from the Zapatista revolt to the Seattle World Trade Organization (WTO) protests, scholars have found examples of political activity that would have been impossible in the pre-Internet era.[8] In these accounts, large, loose coalitions of citizens are able to use the Internet and related technologies to organize themselves with breathtaking speed. Some have seen these examples as proof that the Internet is "disintermediating" political activity, allowing for greater organizational flexibility while radically diminishing the role of political elites.

But if most scholars now agree that the Internet is allowing new forms of political organizing, there has been disagreement about the importance of these changes. Some have argued that citizen disinterest in politics will short-circuit much of the Internet's potential political impact. Using longitudinal data, M. Kent Jennings and Vicki Zeitner (2003) found that Internet use had little effect on civic engagement. Pippa Norris argued that the Internet "probably has had the least impact on changing the motivational basis for political activism" (2001, 22). Markus Prior (2007) found divergent effects depending on one's political engagement: Internet use increased political knowledge among citizens already interested in politics, but had the opposite effect among the previously apathetic. Bruce Bimber similarly concludes that despite some organizational innovations, "it does not appear, at least so far, that new technology leads to higher aggregate levels of political participation" (2003a, 5).

Others disagree. Caroline Tolbert and Ramona McNeal (2003) argue that controlling for other factors, those with access to the Internet and online political news were more likely to report that they voted in the 1996 and 2000 elections. Brian Krueger (2002) similarly suggests that the In-

---

[8] On the reorganization of Environmental Defense (formerly the Environment Defense Fund), see Bimber 2000. On the emergence of MoveOn, see Kahn and Kellner 2004; Chadwick 2006. Scholarship on the Zapatista movement includes Castells 2000; Garrido and Halavais 2003; Cleaver 1998; but see May 2002. For analysis of the Seattle WTO protests, see Bennett 2003ba; Rheingold 2003; Smith 2001.

ternet will indeed mobilize many previously inactive citizens. Some scholars also conclude that at least for younger citizens, Internet use is associated with increased social capital (Shah, Kwak, and Holbert 2001; Shah, McLeod, and Yoon 2001; Johnson and Kaye 2003).

The data and analysis that this book offers is thus relevant to many different lines of research. Yet this book particularly hopes to address recent scholarship that, despite long-standing concerns, concludes that the Internet *is* giving ordinary citizens greater voice in public discourse. These scholars acknowledge the continuing effects of the digital divide, the influence of economic forces and Internet gatekeepers, and the simple fact that all Web sites are not created equal. But as Yochai Benkler observes, "We need to consider the attractiveness of the networked public sphere not from the perspective of the mid-1990s utopianism, but from the perspective of how it compares to the actual media that have dominated the public sphere in all modern democracies" (2006, 260). Richard Rogers opts for a similar stance, suggesting that despite its limitations, the Web should be seen as "the finest candidate there is for unsettling informational politics," offering greater exposure to alternate political viewpoints not aired on the evening news (2004, 3). The growth of blogging in particular has inspired hope. Andrew Chadwick states that "the explosion of blogging has democratized access to the tools and techniques required to make a political difference through content creation" (2006, 129). While Daniel Drezner and Henry Farrell note that some blogs garner far more readership than others, they state that "ultimately, the greatest advantage of the blogosphere is its accessibility" (2004b, 40).

This book will return to Benkler's arguments about what he terms "the networked public sphere"—partly because his *The Wealth of Networks* is an important work in its own right, and partly because Benkler provides an admirably clear digest of similar claims made by others. I will suggest that such accounts suffer from two different types of problems. First, key empirical claims about online political communities do not match up with the data this book provides. For example, Benkler claims that "clusters of moderately read sites provide platforms for a vastly greater number of speakers than are heard in the mass-media audience"; "As the clusters get small enough," Benkler states, "the obscurity of sites participating in the cluster diminishes, while the visibility of superstars remains high, forming a filtering and transmission backbone for universal uptake and local filtering" (2006, 242, 248; see also Drezner and Farrell

2004a). As this book shows, the "moderately read" outlets that trickle-up theories of online discourse rely on are in short supply on every level of the Web.

Second, even to the extent that the Internet or the blogosphere *does* work the way that Benkler and others suppose, Internet politics seems to nurture some democratic values at the expense of others. If our primary concern is the commercial biases of traditional media organizations, or the need for a strong corps of citizen watchdogs, then online politics may indeed promote positive change. Yet it is crucial to remember that democratic politics has other goals, too. No democratic theorist expects citizens' voices to be considered exactly equally, but all would agree that pluralism fails whenever vast swaths of the public are systematically unheard in civic debates. The mechanisms of exclusion may be different online, but this book suggests that they are no less effective.

Gatekeeping, Filtering, and Infrastructure

For many of the observers above, from Benkler to Williams, Hewitt to Trippi, the Internet's most important political impacts come from the elimination of "old media" gatekeepers. The concept of gatekeeping itself is credited to sociologist Kurt Lewin (1947) who suggested that social "channels" often had many points at which "gatekeepers" filtered out some items, while other items were allowed to pass. Initially applied to the food supply (where food products faced a gauntlet of gatekeepers from farmers all the way to households), Lewin pointed out that the theory could be especially helpful in explaining information flow.

The framework of gatekeeping was quickly applied to the study of media. David White's famous study (1950) of a newspaper editor, introduced pseudonymously as "Mr. Gates," looked at the criteria by which wire service stories were deemed "newsworthy" enough to appear in a local newspaper (see also P. Snider 1967). Later media gatekeeping research de-emphasized the judgment (and prejudices) of individual editors, and focused on broader institutional, economic, and structural factors to explain which content was produced, and which stories were printed or broadcast (Gans 1980; Epstein 1974; Fishman 1980).

In recent years, Internet researchers have revived the rubric of gatekeeping. Some argue that commercial Web sites play an important role as filters and "traffic cops" (Hargittai 2000; Cornfield and Rainie 2003; Connolly-Ahern, Williams, and Kaid 2003; Curtin 2000). Other scholars make contrary claims. For example, Bruce Williams and Michael Delli Carpini (2000) declare that new media "undermine the idea that there are discrete gates through which political information passes: if there are no gates, there can be no gatekeepers" (61).

This book argues that gates and gatekeepers remain a critical part of the information landscape, even in the Internet age. Some ways in which online information is filtered are familiar, as traditional news organizations and broadcast companies are prominent on the Web. Other aspects of online filtering are novel. Search engines and portal Web sites are an important force, yet a key part of their role is to aggregate thousands of individual gatekeeping decisions made by others. Ultimately, this book argues that the Internet is not eliminating exclusivity in political life; instead, it is shifting the bar of exclusivity from the *production* to the *filtering* of political information.

In this vein, I want to conclude this introductory chapter by stressing two related themes that underlie much of what is to come. First, if we want to understand online gatekeeping, we need to begin by taking a closer look at the infrastructure of the Internet. Second, when considering political speech online, we must be mindful of the difference between speaking and being heard.

The Infrastructure of the Internet

From the start, claims that new media would weaken or eliminate gate-keepers focused on the Internet's architecture. From Bill Gates's best-selling *Business at the Speed of Thought* to more academic titles such as Nicholas Negroponte's *Being Digital* and Andrew Shapiro's *The Control Revolution,* the presumption was that the biggest changes in both politics and business would come from a host of new entrants who took advantage of lowered barriers to entry. Small, marginal interests and minor political parties were considered particularly likely to be advantaged by the open architecture of the Internet.

Of course, the architecture of the Internet does tell us much about the possibilities of the medium. Yet the understanding of the Internet's in-frastructure that has pervaded most discussions of the medium is incomplete. The various pieces that make up the architecture of the Web function as a whole—and that system is only as open as its most narrow choke point.

I will be referring to infrastructure a great deal, so it is worth taking the time to define the term. In its most general sense, infrastructure refers to the subordinate parts of a more complex system or organization.[9] The word infrastructure was first used in military contexts. In order to field an effective fighting force, one needs not just infantry and tanks but also a network of supporting buildings, installations, and improvements, such as bases, supply depots, railroad bridges, training camps, and so on. Collectively, these supporting facilities came to be known as infrastructure. It remains conventional wisdom that the infrastructure that supplies and knits together an army is often more important than the combat units themselves. A popular aphorism among military personnel is that "amateurs study tactics; professionals study logistics."

For the purposes of this book, I will be talking about infrastructure in two distinct senses. First of all, I will be talking about the infrastructure of communications technologies. In its broadest sense, the infrastructure of the Internet could be said to encompass a great deal: the computers, wiring, and other hardware; the network protocols that allow nodes on the network to talk to one another; the software code that runs the individual computers; the electric grid that powers these machines; or even the schooling that allows users to read and create online text.

I do not intend to analyze every technology and social activity that undergirds Internet use. My goal, rather, is to describe a few key parts of the Internet infrastructure that constrain citizens' choices and ultimately filter the content that citizens see. It remains common to speak of the millions of Web sites online that citizens can choose to visit. Some scholars have talked about personalized information preferences, worrying that citizens will consciously choose to not see some categories of content and some sources of information (Sunstein 2001; Shapiro 1999; Negroponte 1995).

But the most important filtering, I argue, is not conscious at all; it is rather a product of the larger ecology of online information. The link structure of the Web is critical in determining what content citizens see.

---

[9] The *Oxford English Dictionary* defines infrastructure as "a collective term for the subordinate parts of an undertaking; substructure, foundation." Similarly, *Merriam-Webster* defines infrastructure as "the underlying foundation or basic framework (as of a system or organization)."

Links are one way that users travel from one site to another; all else being equal, the more paths there are to a site, the more traffic it will receive. The pattern of links that lead to a site also largely determines its rank in search engine results.

Because of the infrastructure of the Internet, then, not all choices are equal. Some sites consistently rise to the top of Yahoo!'s and Google's search results; some sites never get indexed by search engines at all. The visibility of political content on the Internet follows winners-take-all patterns, with profound implications for political voice. If we abstract away these underlying parts of how citizens interact with the Internet, it is easy to overlook the real patterns in who gets heard online.

In recent years, scholars such as Lawrence Lessig (1999) have argued that if we are to understand the social implications of this technology, we must take a broader view of what the Internet's infrastructure includes. Regulation of the Internet, Lessig and others maintain, happens not just through laws and norms but through the fundamental design choices that went into building the Internet, and through the software code that often determines what users are and are not allowed to do.

One key contention of this book is that our understanding of the technological architecture of the Internet needs to be broader still. The network protocols that route data packets around the Internet and the HTML code used to create Web pages say nothing about search engines, and yet these tools now guide (and powerfully limit) most users' online search behavior. The technological specifications allow hyperlinks to point anywhere on the Web, yet in practice social processes have distributed them in winners-take-all patterns. If we consider the architecture of the Internet more broadly, we find that users' interactions with the Web are far more circumscribed than many realize, and the circle of sites they find and visit is much smaller than is often assumed. All of this changes our conclusions about how much room there is online for citizens' voices.

The Infrastructure of Politics

The other way in which the notion of infrastructure is useful, I suggest, is in reconceptualizing the ways in which the Internet impacts U.S. politics. In popular coverage of the Internet's effects on business, a few online retailers such as Amazon.com or Ebay have gotten much of the attention. Yet behind these online behemoths there is a less glamorous but more important story. For every Amazon or eBay, hundreds of businesses have quietly used the Internet and related information technologies to stream-line operational logistics and generally make business processes more efficient.[10] The greatest impacts of the Internet have been at the back end of business—not storefronts but supply chains.

I suggest that the impact of the Internet on political practice is likely to mirror the Internet's impact on business practices. The Internet does seem to be changing the processes and technologies that support mass political participation and guide elite strategy. Part of the claim here is that chang-ing the *infrastructure* that supports participation can alter the *patterns* of participation. E-mail appeals or text messages, for example, may inspire a different set of citizens to contribute than those who give in response to direct mail.

Early visions of how the Internet would alter campaigning imagined large numbers of ordinary citizens visiting campaign Web sites, engaging in online discussions, using this unmediated information as a basis for political decision making. Thus far the reality has been different. Most of those who visit campaign Web sites are partisans (Bimber and Davis 2003; Howard 2005; Foot and Schneider 2006). The most successful campaign sites to date have acknowledged this fact, using their online presence to solicit funds and volunteers, not to sway undecided voters.

The Difference between Speaking and Being Heard

Discussions of gatekeeping and Internet infrastructure highlight a crucial distinction that needs to be made regarding political voice. As we have seen, many continue to assume that the Internet allows motivated citizens, for the first time, the potential to be heard by a worldwide audience. Debates about blogging provide many recent examples of this assumption in action. Klein, Brokaw, and numerous others have accepted the notion that blogs have expanded ordinary citizens' voice in politics, and have moved on to a discussion of whether this change is good or bad for U.S. democracy.

Yet this book argues that such conclusions are premature. This study is careful to consider who speaks and who gets heard as two separate

---

[10] For economists' treatments of this phenomenon, see Littan and Rivlin 2001; Borenstein and Saloner 2001; Lucking-Reiley and Spulber 2001; Brynjolfsson and Hitt 2000.

questions. On the Internet, the link between the two is weaker than it is in almost any other area of political life.

In this respect, the Internet diverges from much of what political scientists have grown to expect from the literature on political behavior. In many avenues of political participation, scholars have noted that once the initial barriers to participation are overcome, citizens' voices get considered relatively equally. When citizens vote, each ballot carries the same weight in deciding an election. When citizens volunteer for a political campaign or an advocacy group, they all face similar limits; at the extremes, no volunteer has more than twenty-four hours a day to contribute toward a campaign. The greatest exception to this rule has been political fund-raising; among the relatively small set of citizens who donate to political campaigns and interest groups, disparities in wealth make some citizens' voices much louder than others.[11] Even here, though, there are important (albeit imperfect) limits that constrain inequalities in who gets heard. Under federal election law, no citizen could donate more than $2,000 total to any one candidate over the course of the 2003–4 election cycle.[12]

A central claim of this book is that direct political speech on the Internet—by which I mean the posting of political views online by citizens—does not follow these relatively egalitarian patterns. If we look at citizens' voices in terms of the *readership* their postings receive, political expression online is orders of magnitude more unequal than the disparities we are used to in voting, volunteer work, and even political fund-raising. This book also shows that by the most commonly used social science metrics, online audience concentration equals or exceeds that found in most traditional media.

This is not the conclusion I expected when I began this research several years ago. Other scholars may also find these conclusions counterintuitive. It is indeed true that the amount of material available online is vast. In chapter 3, in the first large-scale survey of political content online, my

[11] As Verba, Schlozman, and Brady write, "When we investigated the extent of participatory distortions for a series of politically relevant characteristics, in each case we found it to be markedly greater for contributions than for other forms of activity" (1995, 512).

[12] Individual contribution limits are now adjusted for inflation in odd-numbered years; for the 2007–8 election cycle, donations are capped at $2,300. Contribution limits have never been completely effective, and new tactics—such as donating money to independent "527" political groups—have emerged even as some older loopholes have been closed.

collaborators and I downloaded and analyzed millions of Web pages on half a dozen diverse political topics. Even these methods likely capture only a small fraction of all content on these issues. And yet despite—or rather because of—the enormity of the content available online, citizens seem to cluster strongly around the top few information sources in a given category. The broad patterns of who gets heard online, I suggest, are nearly impossible to miss.

Too often, normative debates about the Internet have gotten ahead of the evidence. Deductive arguments based on a faulty empirical foundation have been more distracting than enlightening. But if this book leaves many normative questions about the Internet's political effects unanswered, I hope that it will help reframe ongoing debates. If the question is, Is the Internet good for U.S. politics? then the answer may well be yes. If the Web has somewhat equalized campaign giving across economic classes, most democratic theorists will applaud. Similarly, in an era where many scholars have worried about declines in civic participation, evidence that online tools can mobilize previously inactive citizens will be welcomed.[13] The Internet has made basic information on countless political subjects accessible to any citizen skilled and motivated enough to seek it out. Blogs and other online forums may help strengthen the watchdog function necessary for democratic accountability.

Yet when we consider direct political speech—the ability of ordinary citizens to have their views considered by their peers and political elites—the facts bear little resemblance to the myths that continue to shape both public discussion and scholarly debate. While it is true that citizens face few formal barriers to posting their views online, this is openness in the most trivial sense. From the perspective of mass politics, we care most not about who posts but about who gets read—and there are plenty of formal and informal barriers that hinder ordinary citizens' ability to reach an audience. Most online content receives no links, attracts no eyeballs, and has minimal political relevance. Again and again, this study finds powerful hierarchies shaping a medium that continues to be celebrated for its openness. This hierarchy is structural, woven into the hyperlinks that make up the Web; it is economic, in the dominance of companies like Google, Yahoo! and Microsoft; and it is social, in the small group of white, highly

---

[13] For an excellent, comprehensive overview of the many studies on declining civic participation, see Macedo et al. 2005.

educated, male professionals who are vastly overrepresented in online opinion. Google and Yahoo! now claim to index tens of billions of online documents; hierarchy is a natural and perhaps inevitable way to organize the vastness of online content. But these hierarchies are not neutral with respect to democratic values.

Understanding the subtle and not-so-subtle ways in which the hierarchies of online life impact politics will be an important task in the twenty-first century. The Internet has served to level some existing political inequalities, but it has also created new ones.

Two

The Lessons of Howard Dean

Not only are we going to New Hampshire, we're going to
South Carolina and Oklahoma and Arizona and North
Dakota and New Mexico, and we're going to California and
Texas and New York. And we're going to South Dakota and
Oregon and Washington and Michigan. And then we're
going to Washington, D.C., to take back the White House!
Yeeaarrhhh!

—Howard Dean, January 19, 2004

If we want to understand how the Internet is changing the political voice of
citizens, there's no better place to start than with Dean, whose name remains synonymous with Internet politics. This is one case, I argue, where
the conventional wisdom is correct. The evidence for the Internet's influence on the Dean campaign is even stronger than many have supposed.
The rise and fall of Dean's candidacy shows us much about what the Internet can do for candidates—and what it cannot.

Dean's meteoric path through the 2004 presidential primaries seems in
some ways predictable. Long-standing political science wisdom suggests several explanations for Dean's ultimate defeat: the central issue of electability,
which seemed to weigh heavily against his campaign; the fact that primary
voters are more moderate than party activists; and the well-documented
difficulty of regaining lost momentum. Less systematic factors—such as numerous verbal gaffes and one infamous scream—surely contributed as well.

Still, the Dean campaign exposes a curious gap in political science
knowledge. If Dean's failure now seems unsurprising, how are scholars
to explain his brief but remarkable success? Though Dean entered the
race a relative unknown, he shattered previous fund-raising records, won
numerous key endorsements, from Al Gore's to the AFL-CIO's, and had a
strong plurality in the polls in the months leading up to the Iowa caucuses.

If we want to understand Dean's early and unexpected rise as the
Democratic front-runner, we should begin by considering one obvious

difference between 2004 and previous primary campaigns: the role of the Internet. Dean's use of the Web to organize, invigorate, and finance his campaign has been much celebrated, but it remains too little understood.

This chapter attempts to reconcile Dean's experience with standard political science views on primary campaigns. Two themes emerge. First, previous scholarship on presidential primaries, which emphasizes the importance of momentum, needs to be viewed in light of the Web's political demographics. Although liberals and conservatives are online in roughly equal numbers, survey data suggest that liberals visit political Web sites much more than do moderates or conservatives. This likely helped Dean by making the online campaign, in essence, an early primary among a very liberal constituency.

Second, the Dean campaign marked an ongoing shift in how candidates use the Web. In the business world, as noted earlier, the Internet's real successes have been not in retail but at the back end: thousands of businesses have quietly used the Internet to streamline organizational logistics. Dean's example suggests that the Web may alter the infrastructure of politics in a similar fashion. Dean used the Internet to revamp back-end campaign functions such as fund-raising and volunteer recruitment—critical tasks that did *not* involve mass appeals to voters. In ways both large and small, Dean's case does not fit with what political scientists think they know about primary dynamics, political recruitment, patterns of political giving, elite strategy, and even the so-called digital divide.

The Liberal Medium?

In covering the Dean campaign, the popular press consistently stressed the novelty of its tactics. Dean did something that was smart, brave, and unprecedented—something that only a candidate with little to lose would do: he created a genuinely interactive campaign Web site. Previous online campaigns—including those of John McCain and Jesse Ventura, the most celebrated antecedents to Dean's efforts—kept rigid control over their Web presence.[1] Encouraging supporters to generate their own content,

---

[1] For a discussion of the ways in which Web site interactivity can reduce positive impressions of a candidate, see Stromer-Galley 2000; Sundar, Kalyanaraman, and Brown 2003. On Ventura's campaign more generally, see Lentz 2001.

join online discussions, create their own Dean sites, and even organize their own events necessarily meant that the campaign gave up some control over the messages it projected. In considering what Dean means for the future of digital politics, I should begin by acknowledging that many campaigns will not follow this lead. Strong candidates have little incentive to take such chances.

Still, Dean's digital innovations are inadequate to explain his successes. To understand what happened during the course of the 2004 primaries, we must look more closely at those who use the Web for political purposes. Online politics, it seems, has a puzzlingly liberal character.

As I noted above, it was clear from the beginning that Web access and usage patterns closely tracked existing social cleavages. The rich and educated used the Internet more than those with less money and education; women lagged behind men; Hispanics and African Americans trailed their white and Asian counterparts. Though most of these gaps in usage have narrowed in recent years—particularly gender differences—large disparities remain.[2] Indeed, as scholars have looked beyond mere access to the Internet and focused on essential user skills, these disparities appear to be as profound as ever.[3]

For political scientists, the demographics of Web users have seemed consistent with a familiar and disturbing pattern. In *Voice and Equality*, for example, Verba, Schlozman, and Brady (1995) argue that differences in political resources result in a systematic distortion in the perceived preferences of the public, and that this distortion favors traditionally privileged groups and those with conservative views. If the Internet is itself an important political resource—a powerful tool for political organizing, fundraising, and information gathering—placing the new medium disproportionately in the hands of advantaged groups might perpetuate or even exacerbate a conservative bias in U.S. politics.

Yet survey data seem to tell a different story. To illustrate this, I turn to the 2000 and 2002 General Social Survey (GSS), the first large-scale surveys to combine measures of Web usage with metrics of users' political and social views. The GSS, which asks respondents to place themselves on a seven-point scale from "very liberal" to "very conservative," shows no

---

[2] On the current dimensions of the digital divide, see Dijk 2005; Warschauer 2004; NTIA 2002; Lenhart et al. 2003.

[3] On this point, see Hargittai 2003; Mossberger, Tolbert, and Stansbury 2003.

Table 2.1
Visits to Political Web Sites by User Ideology

	None	1–2 times	3–4 times	> 5 times	Total
Liberals	62%	20%	7%	11%	291
Moderates	74%	17%	6%	4%	344
Conservatives	69%	19%	7%	5%	327
Total	659	179	63	61	962

This table presents 2000 and 2002 GSS data on the number of visits to political Web sites, broken down by self-reported political attitudes. It shows that liberals are, in general, significantly more likely to visit political Web sites than moderates or conservatives. The most striking finding concerns those who report visiting political Web sites more than five times in the previous thirty days: liberals are more than twice as likely as conservatives to report visiting a political Web site over that period.

liberal-conservative difference between the political leanings of users and nonusers. Nevertheless, although the political ideology of Web users mirrors that of the general population, the two groups have starkly different usage patterns.

Liberals dominate the audience for politics online. Across a wide range of politically relevant activities, from gathering news online to visiting government Web sites, liberals outpace conservatives by a wide margin. As seen in tables 2.1 and 2.2, the results are particularly dramatic for visits to political Web sites, where more than twice as many liberals as conservatives fall into the highest category of Web use.

Primary campaigns are an intraparty phenomenon, and what is true of users generally is also true of Democratic partisans. Among self-identified Democrats, frequent visitors to political Web sites are dramatically more liberal than the party as a whole; they are more highly educated than the general public; and while voters as a group skew older, those who visit political Web sites are disproportionately young.

In Dean's case, the importance of these skewed political demographics is clear. In the early campaign, Dean positioned himself to the left of most competitors. Dean declared that he represented "the Democratic wing of the Democratic party" (quoted in Nagourney 2003) and offered forceful opposition to the Iraq war while other competitors adopted more nuanced positions. If the patterns of political Web use were reversed—if conservatives visited political sites far more than liberals—Dean would have raised less money online, recruited fewer volunteers, and attracted less positive press coverage of his online efforts.

Table 2.2
Frequency of Visits to Political Web Sites

	Model A Coeff. Std. Err	Model B Coeff. Std. Err
Extremely liberal	.72*** (.21)	.70*** (.21)
Liberal	.33*** (.12)	.30** (.16)
Slightly liberal	.32*** (.13)	.28* (.16)
Slightly conservative	.10 (.12)	−.03 (.16)
Conservative	.17 (.12)	.11 (.12)
Extremely conservative	.23 (.24)	.32 (.25)
Years of education	0	.04*** (.02)
Income	0	−.00 (.02)
Age	0	.00 (.00)
Female	0	−.17*** (.08)
Black	0	−.08 (.15)

This table presents ordered probit models of the frequency of visits to political Web sites. The ordinal dependent variable is constructed from answers to the question, In the past thirty days, how often have you visited a Web site for political information? There are 4 categories: $1 =$ never; $2 = 1$–2 times; $3 = 3$–5 times. $4 =$ more than 5 times. * denotes $P < .10$, ** denotes $P < .05$, and *** denotes $P < .01$. Self-described moderates are the base category.

These findings force us to consider whether Dean's experience might be part of a broader, longer-term trend in online activism that benefits Democrats and those with liberal views. Unfortunately, we cannot use subsequent iterations of the GSS to track the evolving ideological profile of those who visit political Web sites. The 2004 GSS respondents questioned about their political Web usage were not asked about their liberal-conservative leanings; the 2006 GSS subjects were not asked about their political Web usage at all.

The 2004 GSS, however, does ask respondents how closely they identify themselves with the Democratic and Republican parties. While less useful in assessing intraparty contests like the presidential primaries, party identification does predict voting behavior better than liberal-conservative self-placement (Miller and Shanks 1996). The two measures are correlated but not interchangeable, producing a correlation coefficient of 0.38 in the 2002 GSS data; more citizens identify themselves with a political party than are willing to describe themselves as something other than an ideological moderate. Though decades-long debates about the meaning and measurement of party identification persist, much evidence suggests that citizens' party identification is more stable (or at least more precisely measured) than their liberal-conservative self-placement (Green, Palmquist, and Schickler 2002; Franklin 1992).

The 2004 GSS was in the field during February, March, and April—after the results in Iowa and New Hampshire, and after hundreds of print and broadcast stories about online campaigning. It thus likely tells us more about the *effects* of the Dean phenomenon than about its *causes*. Duplicating the analysis above in the 2004 sample, using party identification instead of liberal-conservative self-placement, still shows a leftward skew in Web usage. As expected, strong Democrats are significantly more likely to visit political Web sites; yet so are strong Republicans, though by a smaller margin. Those who identify strongly with the Republican Party show larger and more consistent advantages in political Web usage than ideological conservatives did in the preceding analysis.

The biggest usage gaps come among weak partisans and leaning independents. Compared to "true" independents—those who, when pressed, do not admit to leaning toward one party or the other—Democratic-leaning independents and weak Democrats show significantly higher levels of political Web usage. Republican-leaning independents and weak Republicans, by contrast, are not significantly different from true independents. Replacing the dummy variables for each partisan category with a sevenpoint party identification scale, as in model B, similarly shows a Democratic advantage in political usage. Later chapters confirm the findings seen in this survey data, and show that liberal sites attract dramatically greater levels of traffic than conservative ones do.

Should we expect this liberal-conservative gap to be temporary or an enduring feature of the online political landscape? There is some reason to expect that conservatives and Republicans will catch up. The Internet is still a young medium, and effective methods of online organizing arguably remain experimental. As user sophistication continues to improve, as Republican candidates invest resources in exploiting the Web, and as conservative partisans themselves see online participation as a key part of political activism, online politics may have less of a liberal cast.

Ideological and partisan differentials in usage may not fade quickly, though. The year 2004 was not 1994; the majority of the U.S. public had been online for several years before Dean started his run for the presidency. There is no liberal-conservative or Democrat-Republican gap in access more generally, or in time spent online. Moreover, many other mediums of political outreach have had a persistent partisan character. For example, direct mail solicitation has long been a more effective tool for Republicans than for Democrats.

"Big Mo' " Meets the Internet

Liberal overrepresentation online dovetails with a larger point about the dynamics of the primary process. The concept of momentum enjoys a central place in the scholarship on presidential primaries. The snowball effects of early success (or failure) are substantial: candidates who win the first primaries receive more favorable press coverage, more public interest in the campaign, more volunteers, and more money. The order of these contests is thus critical. For example, as Larry Bartels shows, it was "pure, unadulterated luck" that states most favorable to Gary Hart—overwhelmingly white states without major urban populations—were first on the 1984 electoral calendar (1988, 260). The Iowa and New Hampshire results greatly magnified the seriousness of Hart's challenge to Walter Mondale.[4]

Dean's candidacy benefited enormously from a digital version of the Hart effect. In June 2003, the leading liberal activist group MoveOn.org sponsored what it termed an "online primary." Dean won, receiving a 44 percent plurality. The symbolism of the win was appropriate; in a larger sense, the entire online campaign came to serve as a sort of virtual primary. Dean's demonstrable successes on the Web generated the sort of coverage, enthusiasm, and compounded success that candidates usually enjoy only after winning an actual electoral contest.

---

[4] See especially chapter 10 in Bartels 1988.

Dean's Internet campaign produced a spiral of positive press coverage. A Lexis-Nexis search finds 1,325 stories in major papers that mentioned Dean's Internet success during the six months preceding the New Hampshire primary—a priceless publicity boon for a candidate who began as a dark horse. Both the scale of Dean's online organization and his unprecedented success at raising large amounts of money in small donations seemed to qualify as newsworthy. Dean's campaign provided other tangible metrics of success: the long list of supportive blogs, the number of hits on its own home page, the number of Dean house parties, and the number of citizens willing to sign up as supporters on the Dean Web site. Overall, the strength of Dean's online organization was taken as evidence that Dean had broad grassroots support.

Dean was not the only beneficiary. General Wesley Clark, whose late entry shook up the primary contest, witnessed a similar effect. Though Clark's online efforts were smaller than Dean's, they nonetheless outpaced the rest of the field. Clark raised $17 million, much of it online—far less than Dean's $52 million, but raised over a shorter time span (CRP 2004). And while Clark did not have the extensive network of bloggers that Dean relied on, he did make good use of both his campaign Web site and other online tools. As with Dean, the press counted these online victories as pro-Clark momentum, citing them as evidence of grassroots support and the campaign's financial robustness. The 2004 Internet campaign thus became in an important sense the earliest primary. At the same time, those who visit political Web sites are a constituency like no other.

Dean's example shows that it is possible to translate online interest into tangible political resources—money, positive press coverage, and volunteers. It also reveals that the Web can grant a partly intangible asset: early momentum.

The Internet and the Infrastructure of Politics

Overall, then, the Dean campaign suggests that political behavior in the online world follows unexpected fault lines. There is a second lesson to be drawn: the Internet may alter key parts of the nation's political infrastructure. Dean's example indicates that the Web's evolution in the business world, where business-to-business has had larger impacts than business-to-consumer, is being repeated in the political realm.

Initially, most candidates tailored their Web sites to reach swing voters, independents, and the undecided—the elusive median voter. This strategy produced dismal results. Survey data show that most political Web site visitors are not swing voters but rather those with strong party affiliations and strong preexisting views on politics (Bimber and Davis 2003; Foot and Schneider 2006). Traffic to most campaign sites has been a trickle, and (at least until the Dean phenomenon) campaign managers commonly saw the Internet as merely a sideshow to the "real" campaign. Bruce Bimber and Richard Davis thus conclude, in one of the best studies of digital campaigning, that the Web will have modest effects on mass politics.

Bimber and Davis are right that online campaigning thus far consists of "preaching to the converted." Yet increasingly, Dean and other candidates have turned this fact to their advantage. Instead of online appeals to the median voter, a new breed of campaign Web site has sought to engage and motivate those most likely to become core supporters. If Web sites are not a way to reach the masses, the Dean campaign and others have shown that they can be a powerful tool for energizing the faithful and fundraising. In short, the Dean phenomenon demonstrates that the Internet can affect what might be termed the supply chain of politics.

Back-end logistics are a critical component of candidate strategy and the locus of many types of political activity. The gap between prevailing theory and Dean's experience is particularly significant for fund-raising and the recruitment of volunteers. Focusing our attention on these two areas, I ask: What would have happened to the Dean campaign without the Internet?

Internet Fund-raising

Prior to Dean's example, it was commonplace to downplay the importance of the Internet for campaign fund-raising (see, for example, Ward, Nixon, and Gibson 2003, 20; Cornfield and Rainie 2003). Bill Clinton's 1996 campaign had raised only $10 thousand online (Davis 1998, 109). While some early survey data suggested that campaign giving was one of the few political activities affected by Internet use (Bimber 2001), the amount of money raised online remained modest. In the 2000 primary season, Gore and Bush reportedly raised only $2.7 and $1.6 million, respectively; McCain reportedly raised $1.4 million in the three days following his victory in the New Hampshire primary (Bimber and Davis 2003, 39). Yet even these sums are likely an exaggeration, as the 2000 presidential campaigns routinely laundered contributions from fund-raising events and telephone donations through their Web sites, in order to inflate their online totals and generate press coverage of their ostensible online success (Bimber 2003a, 183–84).

Against this backdrop, Dean's Internet fund-raising was both surprising and hugely important. For candidates in presidential primaries, the ability to raise funds is a prerequisite to being taken seriously, and no previous candidate of either party had successfully translated two-digit donations into real money. By the end of January 2004, as the primaries commenced, Dean had raised more than $41 million, roughly half of that online; 318,884 citizens had contributed to the Dean campaign.[5] Overall, 61 percent of Dean's financial resources came from those giving $200 or less. Only 2,851 donors—less than 1 percent of the total—gave $2,000, the maximum under federal law. These large givers provided 11 percent of Dean's total funds.

The distribution of giving for the Dean campaign was almost exactly the reverse of his rivals. To keep Dean's success in perspective, note that Bush's reelection campaign far exceeded Dean's money-raising efforts, bringing in a total of $130.8 million over the 2003 calendar year alone. By the end of January 2004, 42,649 of Bush's donors had given the federal maximum of $2,000. These large gifts accounted for 68 percent of Bush's total, while donations of less than $200 contributed less than 16 percent of Bush's funding. And though Democratic candidates like Kerry and Edwards raised far less than Bush, their campaigns similarly relied on large donors to get them through the early primaries. At the end of January, those who gave the $2,000 maximum were responsible for 58 percent of Kerry's campaign war chest, and 73 percent of Edwards's financial resources.

The Dean campaign departs from academic expectations in several respects. First, because of the influx of small donors, the less-than-affluent contributed a greater share of Dean's funding than that of any major presidential candidate in the preceding decades. Second, smaller donations send less precise messages to candidates. Verba, Schlozman, and Brady (1995) declare that the power of contributions is the fact that they are both "loud and clear"—money is key to electoral success, and it communicates a great deal about the giver's preferred policies. But the sheer number of citizens

---

[5] All fund-raising figures are from the Center for Responsive Politics (2004).

who donated to the Dean campaign means that the messages were rather soft and indistinct. A hand-delivered $2,000 check communicates more information than forty individual $50 credit card contributions submitted via the campaign Web site. Third, most Internet donations to Dean's campaign were spontaneous. Donating money to a political campaign is traditionally the type of political participation least likely to be self-generated, and personal social contacts play an important role. Most campaign contributions are solicited, and people that the donor already knows are generally the ones who ask for donations (Verb, Schlozman, and Brady 1995, chap. 5). By contrast, Dean's funding came mostly from individuals who sought out the campaign on their own. Dean's success thus forces political scientists to reexamine much of what they think they know about the relationship between money and politics: the demographics and political views of those who give money, how donations are solicited, the clarity with which money communicates preferred policies, and the extent of the rightward preference distortion that political fund-raising induces in U.S. politics.

Networks of Political Recruitment and the Net

Political scientists have often noted that those who participate in politics are those who are asked. The literature on political participation emphasizes the role that social networks and social pressure play in recruitment. Yet if social networks typically serve as gatekeepers in the political process, record numbers of Dean supporters seem to have jumped the fence.

Dean's focus on "meetups"—Web-organized face-to-face meetings of citizens interested in the campaign—was particularly consequential. Meetups proved to be an elegantly simple organizational strategy. On either the official Dean site or the Meetup.com home page, citizens could offer their e-mail address and zip code, and immediately receive e-mail reminders about pro-Dean meetings in their vicinity. The process of signing up for a local Dean meetup could take as little as thirty seconds.

By the time Dean dropped out of the Democratic race, 640,937 people had registered as Dean supporters through the campaign Web site; 188,941 of those had signed up to receive notices about meetings in their area.[6]

---

[6] Data on the total number of supporters are from the Dean Web site (http://www.deanfor america.com). Data on the number of Dean supporters registered for meetups are from Meetup .com.

According to Meetup.com's attendance figures, more than 40 percent of these supporters—about 75,000 people—actually attended a meeting. Dean meetups were organized in 612 cities. As one of the founders of a state Dean organization declared, "We always considered the meetups to be our primary recruiting tool."[7] Survey data collected from Dean meetup participants in Massachusetts by Christine Williams, Bruce Weinberg, and Jesse Gordon suggest that these gatherings were indeed an effective tool.[8] More than 96 percent of the respondents reported that they wished to become active volunteers after attending a Dean meetup. In both the sheer numbers of those who attended early candidate events and in the wide geographic dispersion of these volunteers, Dean greatly exceeded expectations for an ostensibly minor candidate.

Some popular accounts suggested that Dean's campaign was transforming numerous previously inactive citizens into activists. Trippi (2005, xii) himself remarked on the inexperience of Dean's campaign volunteers. In their October and January surveys, Williams, Weinberg, and Gordon (2004) found that only 39 and 47 percent of their respondents, respectively, had volunteered in previous election cycles. Other scholarly surveys of Dean volunteers found similarly low levels of experience (Klotz 2004; Kohut 2005).

In contrast, most primary campaign volunteers are chronic participators; previous studies have found that for almost every candidate, two-thirds to four-fifths of their primary campaign workers are veterans (see, for example, Johnson and Gibson 1974). Data from the 1988 nominating contest reinforce that conclusion. For every candidate but one, more than two-thirds of their volunteers were previously active as either campaign workers or party officers (Abramowitz et al. 2001). Jesse Jackson's insurgent candidacy in many ways resembles Dean's, but even 72 percent of Jackson's volunteers were veterans. (Pat Robertson's religiously inspired campaign is the only exception; only 35 percent of its volunteers had previous experience.)

Ross Perot's 1992 campaign provides another interesting point of comparison with Dean. Perot used a 1-800 telephone number to solicit volunteers and was credited in popular accounts with recruiting previously

---

[7] Jesse Gordon, cofounder of Mass for Dean, personal communication, February 19, 2004.

[8] Williams, Weinberg, and Gordon 2004; survey data are available online at http://mee-meetupsurvey.com/study/reportsdata.html.

inactive citizens. Nonetheless, data gathered by Ronald Rapoport and Walter Stone (1999) show that more than 67 percent of Perot's volunteers had previous campaign experience; moreover, about a third had been working for George H. W. Bush or Michael Dukakis four years before.

The most surprising finding to emerge from the Williams, Weinberg, and Gordon (2004) data, however, is not that Dean's volunteers were relatively inexperienced but that only 23 percent (October) and 31 percent (January) of the survey respondents learned about meetups from someone they knew. Almost all of the rest found out about the first gathering they attended through the national Dean Web site, the local pro-Dean Web site, or the Meetup.com home page. These figures are a significant departure from the expectations set by previous scholarship. Verba, Schlozman, and Brady (1995), for example, found that more than 80 percent of contacts for campaign recruitment came through personal relationships. According to the civic voluntarism model, ground-level social networks should have been necessary to attract and retain supporters. In Dean's case, these networks were largely absent—yet new technology allowed Dean to create local, decentralized social networks from scratch.

Dean without the Internet: Considering the Counterfactual

I have so far offered a causal explanation for Dean's initial rise as the Democratic Party front-runner. In social science, causal questions are ultimately about counterfactuals. Thus, it is worth putting these observations together to ask, But for the Internet, how should we have expected Dean's campaign to unfold? While such analysis is never an exact science, the strong body of established research on participation, fund-raising, and primary politics makes Dean's case study easier than most.

In the 2004 primary field, Dean had several potential advantages over his competitors that would have been important with or without the Internet. Many Dean supporters opposed the war in Iraq, and there was no other staunch antiwar candidate. As both a governor and medical doctor, Dean presented a compelling personal narrative. His energetic presence on the stump (and the fervor of his attacks on the president) contrasted sharply with many of his rivals. For the dark horse candidate, being ignored is the biggest danger; Dean was consistently quotable.

A completely off-line Dean campaign, then, would still have had strengths. But one thing it would not have done is raise more than a fraction of the $52 million that Dean ultimately received. Dean's campaign defied the example of every previous primary candidate, the Republicans' long-standing advantage in small donations, and every political science model about how much candidates raise and from whom. It is not just the grand sums of money raised that point to the influence of the Internet—though that was important enough—but also the balance betweeen large and small donations. The only other recent primary campaigns to raise a substantial percentage of their funding from small donors—specifically Clark's and Dennis Kucinich's—were themselves heavily invested in the Web. Not only that, once Senator Kerry had the nomination, his sudden success in online fund-raising dramatically increased the proportion of funding he received from smaller donors: whereas at the end of January, 58 percent of his money had come from those giving $2,000 each, by the end of June those who gave the maximum accounted for only 34 percent of Kerry's total war chest (CRP 2004).

To get a sense of Dean's expected fund-raising without the Internet, let us make two assumptions for the sake of argument: first, that Dean's online success did not scare off more large donors than it attracted; and second, that without the Internet, large donors would have provided roughly the same proportion of Dean's funding that they did for previous primary candidates or for those of Dean's competitors who failed to run strong Web campaigns. Dean attracted 2,851 donors who gave the $2,000 maximum. Let us conjecture that these donors would otherwise have accounted for 50 percent of Dean's funds—still less than the percentage that they accounted for in the early fund-raising for Bush, Kerry, Edwards, Dick Gephardt, and Joe Lieberman. In that case, Dean would have raised no more than $11 million in campaign funds, or 21 percent of his actual total—placing him behind all of the above candidates in campaign funds.

These facts leave us with only two credible conclusions: either the Internet suddenly made it possible for a few candidates to raise more money in smaller chunks than in the past, or some other change in the political landscape—a change that happened to be correlated with extensive campaign Web use—was responsible. Given that so much of this new funding was received online, Occam's razor suggests that we assign the Internet the causal role.

The second area where Dean's campaign would have unfolded differently concerns his network of volunteers. Comparing Dean's volunteers with the profile of volunteers in previous campaigns suggests that without the meetup phenomenon, Dean's volunteer corps would have been far smaller. Moreover, it would have grown more out of existing interpersonal networks, it would not have been as geographically dispersed, and it would have had proportionally more veterans and fewer previously inactive volunteers.

Finally, the early press coverage that Dean received focused largely on his online success in fund-raising and volunteer recruitment. Without the financial and organizational fruits of the online campaign, much of this coverage would simply not have happened, leaving Dean to struggle with name recognition in a crowded field. And of course, without extensive press coverage to make his campaign credible, Dean would not have won major endorsements.

So where would Dean have been with far less money, with a leaner volunteer organization, and without such ubiquitous (and often glowing) early coverage of his campaign? Not out of the race, probably—with luck, and without the curse of high expectations, strong finishes in Iowa and New Hampshire might have given him a solid base to build on in the later primaries. Nonetheless, without the Internet, it seems impossible that Dean would have become so formidable so early.

The End of the Beginning

For months leading up to the Iowa caucuses, the Dean campaign seemed poised to do for the Internet what the Kennedy-Nixon debate did for television: provide an undeniable demonstration of the new medium's political power. The result proved anticlimactic. In the aftermath of the Dean meltdown, some observers dismissed Dean's candidacy as a failed referendum on the importance of digital politics. Many lessons of the Dean campaign are indeed remedial ones: momentum matters; a candidate's perceived viability and electability matter; candidate gaffes and misstatements matter; and it matters that primary voters have different preferences than party activists. Even the best-funded campaigns are not assured of victory.

But this is not the whole story. In trying to squeeze Dean into established patterns, scholars should not miss the key ways in which he simply doesn't fit. The puzzle for political scientists is not why Dean failed but how he ever become the front-runner in the first place.

My answer to this question is simple: to paraphrase a previous presidential campaign, it's the Internet, stupid. The geographic reach of the Dean campaign, the size of its volunteer corps, and its ability to reach previously inactive citizens were all a result of Dean's Internet strategy. Dean challenges nearly all of the conventional wisdom on political fund-raising: who gives, to whom, how much, and with what sort of underlying message. With the nomination in hand, Kerry suddenly inherited Dean's fund-raising success, raising a stunning $40 million just in the first quarter of 2004 ($26 million of that online) and keeping pace with the Bush fund-raising machine. Kerry ultimately raised $83 million online, more than one-third of his fund-raising total (Justice 2004).

Yet the best evidence that Dean was not a fluke, but rather part of a seismic shift in the U.S. political landscape, comes from the 2008 election cycle. As this book goes to press in early 2008, the race for the Democratic presidential nomination is still undecided, while McCain has clinched the Republican race. Many parts of the campaign are difficult to assess at such an early date, but fund-raising is one area where reliable data are already available. As in the previous election cycle, the Internet has proved to be an especially effective tool for liberal and Democratic candidates. The Republican who was most successful at online fund-raising, Ron Paul, took pro–civil liberties and anti–Iraq war positions not shared by most Republicans. Though Paul's campaign fund-raising started slowly, he ended up collecting $20 million in the last quarter of 2007—more than McCain and Mitt Romney, the next closest Republican candidates, combined (Malcolm 2008). As with Dean, Paul's failures at the ballot box remind us that fund-raising alone does not guarantee electoral success.

The impact of Internet fund-raising on the 2008 election cycle can be seen even more clearly in Obama's campaign. Hillary Clinton and Obama both exceeded previous Democratic fund-raising records, with Clinton collecting $118 million and Obama gathering $103 million over the 2007 calendar year (Wayne and Zeleny 2008). Consistent with established patterns, Clinton raised about half of her 2007 war chest from donors giving the $2,300 maximum, while the biggest donors contributed one-third of Obama's 2007 funding. Even more telling, the portion of Obama's funding coming from donors giving $200 or less grew every quarter in 2007, from 23 percent in the first quarter to 47 percent in the last quarter (Healy and Zeleny 2008). And as primary voting began, Obama's online fund-raising from small donors exploded. In January 2008 alone Obama

Table 2.3
Partisanship and Political Web Site Visits

	Model A Coeff. *Std. Err*	Model B Coeff. *Std. Err*
Strong Democrat	.72***	
	(.17)	0
Weak Democrat	.32*	
	(.17)	0
Democratic-leaning independent	.52***	
	(.20)	0
Republican-leaning independent	.14	
	(.21)	0
Weak Republican	.03	
	(.18)	0
Strong Republican	.50***	
	(.17)	0
Party identification scale		−.06***
	0	(.02)
Years of education	.08***	.08***
	(.02)	(.03)
Income	.03	−.02
	(.02)	(.02)
Age	−.008***	−.006*
	(.003)	(.003)
Female	−.31***	−.30***
	(.10)	(.10)
Black	−.14	−.08
	(.15)	(.15)

This table presents ordered probit models of the frequency of visits to political Web sites, based on 2004 data from the GSS. The ordinal dependent variable is constructed from answers to the question, "In the past thirty days, how often have you visited a Web site for political information?" There are 4 categories: $1 =$ never; $2 = 1$–2 times; $3 = 3$–5 times; and $4 =$ more than 5 times. Independents who do not lean toward one of the two major parties are the base category in Model A. Model B uses a seven-point party ID scale, with lower values equal to stronger ties to the Democratic Party, and higher values a stronger association with Republicans. * denotes $P < .10$, ** denotes $P < .05$, and *** denotes $P < .01$.

raised $36 million, with $28 million of that from online contributions (Luo 2008). Obama raised more online just in January than Dean did in the entire 2004 campaign cycle. Obama's February haul was even larger: $55 million, of which $45 million came from online contributions (Zeleny and Seelye 2008). By the end of February more than one million citizens had contributed to the Obama campaign.

As impressive as Obama's fundraising results are, it is important to emphasize that much of his campaign effort was hardly innovative. The Obama campaign's biggest expenditures were broadcast advertising, paid staff, and travel costs, precisely the same categories that soaked up most of Clinton's campaign spending.[9] Trippi himself, who spent most of the election cycle as a senior adviser to Edwards, noted that Obama's effort relied on a traditional, highly centralized campaign organization, with key strategic decisions made by a handful of experienced aides. Trippi described the Obama campaign as a hybrid operation featuring "command and control at the top while empowering the bottom to make a difference" (quoted in Berman 2008).

The Dean campaign marked the end of the beginning for Internet politics, the moment when the medium impacted traditional concerns like campaign fund-raising and mobilization. Obama's ability to replicate and ultimately surpass Dean's fund-raising makes the task of understanding the Dean's phenomenon even more urgent. After the 2004 and 2008 campaigns, few would contest the claim that the Internet has transformed political giving. Yet whatever the ultimate result of the 2008 presidential contest, Dean's and Obama's examples suggest that the campaign for resources is changing more quickly than the campaign for votes.

---

[9] Analysis of presidential campaign expenditure data from the Center for Responsive Politics, http://opensecrets.org (accessed March 4, 2008).

Three

"Googlearchy": The Link Structure of Political Web Sites

If everyone has a voice, no one really has a voice. Any single
voice will be drowned out by many thousands of "Gee, this
is my blog, I thought it would be a good idea to start one
because my cat is so cute. I'll post pictures of my cat and
I love Jesus."
—User "Dancin Santa," posted on Slashdot.org

In studying political voice, social scientists have examined many types of citizen participation. They have studied who volunteers for political campaigns, who writes letters to their elected representatives, who joins advocacy groups, who donates money to political causes—and of course, which citizens vote, and for whom. It was these traditional political activities along with their online analogues that were the focus of the previous chapter. Dean won the attention of Internet enthusiasts and skeptics alike because his campaign showed that the Internet could impact these long-standing concerns. Every campaign hopes for numerous volunteers; Dean showed that volunteers could be mobilized online. Every campaign wants lots of money; the Internet fueled Dean's fund-raising success.

This focus on traditional areas of political activism is quite correct, as far as it goes. Yet this chapter takes a step back. Claims about the Internet and political voice have concentrated as much on political discourse as on political participation. The recurring suggestion is that the Internet is a "narrowcasting" or "pointcasting" medium that levels the playing field, eliminates traditional gatekeepers, and gives voice to marginalized or resource-poor groups. According to some, even citizens in their sleepwear can be heard in online politics.

Claims about the importance of narrowcasting online have persisted, in part, because they are difficult to test. Such theories argue—rather counterintuitively—that it is not the biggest sites that matter online but rather the smallest. By definition, such sites get so little traffic that their relative importance cannot be accurately measured with survey data. Even the massive, ten-million-subject Hitwise sample used in later chapters is unable to adequately measure traffic patterns at such a microscopic level.

This chapter proposes a new approach to deal with this dilemma. It suggests that if we want to understand how the Internet is (and is not) changing the political landscape, we have to consider a different sort of political behavior: hyperlinking. In the process, it is necessary to rethink certain assumptions about the openness of the Internet.

On the Internet, different layers of hardware and software control everything from where data packets are routed to how many people are allowed to join an AOL chat room. One common schema is to consider the Internet's architecture as three connected layers (Lessig 2001; Benkler 2006). At the lowest level, there is the *hardware layer*, the computing devices and the wiring that connects them. Above that, there is the *code* or *logical layer*, the protocols that transfer data across the network. Lastly, there is the *content layer*, the documents, files, and applications that are served to Internet users. Lessig and others argue that the Internet's architecture is not fixed—and that attempts by commercial and security interests to change the architecture of the Internet threaten the medium's openness.[1]

These scholars are surely correct that we need to take a closer look at the infrastructure of the Internet if we are to understand its social and political effects. Yet a central argument of this book is that our understanding of the Internet's infrastructure needs to be broader. This chapter asserts that the link structure of the Internet is particularly important in shaping online political activity, even though it does not fit well into the traditional "layer cake" description of the Internet's architecture.

Millions of Americans have now created their own blogs or Web sites. Hundreds of thousands of businesses and organizations have followed suit. Creating a link to another Web site hardly conjures up the energetic activity that "activism" assumes, and those linking to other sites may not even be advocating the political views they reference. As this chapter will show, the way in which these Web site owners link to each other is anything but random.

---

[1] In this vein, see Castells 2000; Boyle 1996; Deibert 2000, 2003.

The interlocking patterns that hyperlinks form are the reason the medium was named the Web in the first place. Hyperlinks encode much useful information. Most users see a tangible demonstration of this every day: PageRank, the ranking algorithm that powers the Google search engine, relies largely on the link structure of the Web to order its results. Other search engines, including Yahoo! and Microsoft Search, also focus on link structure. Though they are embedded in the content layer of the Web, hyperlinks in practice have become the backbone of what should probably be considered another, higher layer of Internet architecture: what we might call the *search layer*, which encompasses the various means by which users find and sort online content. With search engine referrals themselves a large fraction of Internet traffic, the tools and methods of searching are arguably just as important as the content itself. And as the history of Google shows, changes in the search layer of the Internet can have dramatic consequences for Web usage, even if the content layer of the Web remains (mostly) unchanged.

The research described in this chapter was performed in collaboration with Kostas Tsioutsiouliklis and Judy Johnson; at the time this research was conducted, both were research scientists at NEC Research Laboratories. We argue that the link structure of the Web can approximate the relative visibility and the relative traffic of political Web sites, even in the communities too small to study with cross-sectional data. The number of links pointing to a site is correlated with both its ranking in search engines and the number of visitors the site ultimately receives. The link topology of the Internet thus allows us to draw a rough map of how the attention of citizens is distributed across different sources of online information.

Tsioutsiouliklis, Johnson, and I use computer science techniques to explore millions of Web pages, looking at topical clusters of sites focused on a variety of subjects: Congress, general politics, abortion, the presidency, the death penalty, and gun control. The distribution of links within each community of sites approximates a power law, where a small set of hypersuccessful sites receives most of the links.

The popular wisdom that the Web functions as a narrowcasting or pointcasting medium is not consistent with these data. Nor are claims that the Internet is dominated by a "long tail," or that online political communities provide "vast" numbers of "moderately read" outlets for citizen debate. The link topology of the Web suggests that the online public sphere is less open than many have hoped or feared.

What Link Structure Can Tell Political Scientists

The structure of the Web has been a fertile area of scholarship in recent years. Though most of this work has been done by computer scientists and applied physicists, the patterns they have found in the apparent chaos of the Web should give political scientists cause to rethink the Web's political implications.

In looking at the structure of the Web, the central finding is that links between sites obey strong statistical regularities. Over the entire Web, the distribution of both inbound and outbound hyperlinks follows a power law or scale-free distribution (Barabási and Albert 1999; Kumar et al. 1999). More precisely, the probability that a randomly selected Web page has K links is proportional to $K^{-\alpha}$ for large K.

Data follow a power law distribution when the size of an observation is inversely and exponentially proportional to its frequency. For example, the distribution of wealth, as Vilfredo Pareto (1897) famously explained, is a power law distribution, where 20 percent of the population controls 80 percent of the wealth. Numerous other social and natural phenomena follow power-law patterns as well, from earthquakes to intracell protein networks, from the size of firms to the size of cities, from the severity of wars to the number of sexual contacts (Huberman 2001; Krugman 1994; Cederman 2003; Liljeros et al. 2001).

As such diverse scholarship demonstrates, power law structures can be generated by very different underlying processes. But in every case, a power law distribution leads to starkly inegalitarian outcomes. Imagine a hypothetical community where wealth is distributed according to a power law. At one end of the spectrum, there is one millionaire, ten individuals worth at least a hundred thousand dollars, a hundred people worth ten thousand dollars, and a thousand people worth at least a thousand dollars. At the opposite end, one million people have a net worth of one dollar. In this hypothetical community, wealth is distributed in proportion to the function $K^{-\alpha}$, where $\alpha = 1$.

In the context of the Web, studies have found the online environment to be far more concentrated even than the hypothetical example above, generating values of $\alpha \approx 2.1$ for inbound hyperlinks and $\alpha \approx 2.7$ for outbound hyperlinks (Kumar et al. 1999; Barabási et al. 2000; Lawrence and Giles 1998; Faloutsos, Faloutsos, and Faloutsos 1999).[2] A few popular sites (such as Yahoo! or AOL or Google) receive a large portion of the total links; less successful sites (such as most personal Web pages) receive hardly any links at all. Traffic, like link structure, follows a power-law distribution with roughly the same parameters (Huberman et al. 1998; Adamic and Huberman 2000). There is thus a small set of sites that receive most of the links, and a small set of sites that receive most online visitors. For the purposes of this chapter, it is important to show that these two groups are one and the same.

My colleagues and I do this in two ways. In the next sections, I explain *why* we should expect the number of links pointing to a site to be a powerful predictor of traffic: both surfing patterns and search engines send users to the sites that have accumulated the most links. Then, we test this expectation by looking at real-world data on the correlation between links and site traffic.

Finding Online Information

In order to visit a Web site, one must be able to find it in the first place. Known sites, or sites found by off-line means, can be visited by typing in the URL or using a bookmark within a Web browser. Social networks can also play a role in directing users to new Web sites; e-mail makes it easy for friends and relatives to recommend sites to one another.

On their own, however, users have only two ways to find previously unknown content. First, content can be discovered by surfing away from known sites; and second, it can be found through online search tools such as Google or the Yahoo! directory service. In both cases, the number of inbound hyperlinks is a crucial determinant of a Web page's visibility.

Much of the association between inbound links and traffic is simple: hyperlinks exist to be followed. The more hyperlinks there are to a given site, the more chances that users on connecting sites have to follow them. In the aggregate, more paths to a site means more traffic.

---

[2] Barabási et al. (2000) and Kumar et al. (1999) seem to disagree on the value of α for outgoing hyperlinks; Barabási et al. propose a value of $\alpha = 2.4$. This scholarship also shows that these parameters have been highly stable over time, even as the Web has undergone explosive growth.

What is true for individual surfers is doubly so for search engines. The first generation of search engines, such as AltaVista, focused on keyword density and other characteristics found within individual Web pages. The Google search engine was a powerful disruptive technology. Google's contribution was to take a broader view, and use the connections *between* Web sites to find the best content. Google founders Sergey Brin and Larry Page (1998) developed PageRank, a recursive algorithm in which sites that receive lots of links, from *other* sites that receive lots of links, are ranked most highly (see also Pandurangan, Raghavan, and Upfal 2002). In essence, sites are ranked in a popularity contest in which each link is a vote, but the votes of popular sites carry more weight.[3]

Both search engines and surfing behavior thus privilege the same sorts of Web pages. Sites that are heavily linked become prominent; most other sites are likely to be ignored.

By July 2006, Google owned 60 percent of the U.S. search engine market.[4] This compared to 23 percent for Yahoo! Search, and 12 percent for MSN Search (Tancer 2006). Over the past several years, Google has steadily taken market share from its rivals. One might think that a less concentrated search engine market would help ensure diversity in the content seen. But once search engines focus on link structure, the popularity contest dynamics seen with PageRank are difficult to avoid. The HITS algorithm is one widely known alternative to PageRank, and uses the mutually reinforcing structure of "hubs" and "authorities" to rank results (Kleinberg 1999; Marendy 2001). Chris Ding and his colleagues (2002) show that despite the fact that the HITS approach is "at the other end of the search engine spectrum" from PageRank, it tends to rank the same set of sites first. Indeed, both algorithms—and any likely competitors—produce results that are hardly different than just ordering sites by the number of inlinks they receive (Ding et al. 2002; Tomlin 2003). (Similarity in search results will be explored in greater detail in the following chapter.)

---

[3] As time has passed, Google has increasingly incorporated other factors into its rating algorithm. Though these refinements make it harder to manipulate search engine results, they make only modest changes in the overall rankings—particularly in the first few pages of search results. As of this writing, PageRank and similar measures of link structure continue to be the backbone of Google's ranking system.

[4] This figure includes Google-powered searches on AOL.com. AOL searches were 7 percent of the total market; with AOL excluded, Google's market share was 53 percent.

The Relation between Inbound Links and Web Traffic

To recap: we know that over the entire Web, both traffic and links are power-law distributed. We also have reason to believe that traffic will be driven to heavily linked sites. But how close is the relationship between link structure and site visits in practice?

Both our own analysis and that of other researchers suggests that the connection is reasonably strong. Lada Adamic of Hewlett-Packard Laboratories provided us with data on links to Web sites along with the number of visitors these sites receive. The site visit data are from a randomly selected, anonymized set of users from a large Internet service provider. They include 120,000 site visits by 60,000 users; the link data for visited sites were compiled by Alexa Corporation.

In these data, the number of inbound links and the number of site visits are highly correlated, generating a correlation coefficient of 0.704. The raw number of hyperlinks pointing to a site does predict much of its traffic. These results seem particularly strong given that the data include advertising links; because the click-through rate on online advertising is notoriously low, advertising sites are heavily linked but lightly visited.[5]

In power-law distributions, a tiny portion of the observations produce most of the variance. We might posit that removing or de-emphasizing the top sites would weaken this correlation. Taking the square root of the data—and thus compressing the difference between the largest and smallest observations—does attenuate the relationship between links and traffic. After taking the root of the data, the correlation coefficient drops to 0.449. Segmenting the data suggests a similar conclusion. If we look at just the top five hundred sites by traffic, the correlation coefficient rises slightly, to 0.726. Yet in the remainder of the data *without* these top five hundred sites, the correlation coefficient is only 0.118.

Link patterns thus seem reasonably good at identifying the small group of heavily trafficked sites. There is far less variance to explain among less popular sites, and here inbound links tell us little about whether a site is likely to receive two visitors or twenty.

Others have similarly suggested a strong connection between links and traffic to blogs. Several sites track the number of links that these online

---

[5] According to the terms under which we received these data, the site URLs were unlabeled; therefore, advertising links could not be omitted from the analysis.

journals receive, and many blogs use Sitemeter.com to track visitors. Using these data, Clay Shirky (2004) found that links and traffic have roughly the same correlation within blogs as in the above data on the Web as a whole. Shirky, too, discovered that links are best at predicting the traffic of popular sites.

All of this returns us to our prior question: How is traffic distributed among political Web sites? While the global power-law distribution of the Internet is clear, subgroups of sites also diverge significantly from the overall pattern. Within specific categories of sites, researchers have found that the hyperlinks are less skewed toward a few dominant sites (Pennock. et al. 2002). Benkler in particular has made much of David Pennock and his colleagues' research, which (like our study) came out of NEC Research Labs. Benkler argues that Pennock and his colleagues' findings support his "Goldilocks" theory that online concentration is "just right." Political content online, Benkler suggests, is just concentrated enough to support "universal uptake and local filtering" (2006, 248).

It is worth emphasizing, however, that even in Pennock and his colleagues' research, communities that follow more egalitarian patterns are the exception rather than the rule. The communities that do not follow winners-take-all hierarchies—for example, sites for publicly listed companies and university home pages—all have one thing in common: they are parasitic on preexisting, real-world social networks. Employees at public companies are familiar with both the largest corporations and companies within their market niche; university scholars recognize both the Harvards and Yales of the educational world as well as their peers at nearby educational institutions. As Albert-László Barabási (2002) notes, this level of horizontal visibility within communities is rare online.

It is thus far from clear that subcategories of political sites should be as egalitarian as Benkler assumes. The only way to understand the structure of political Web sites is to measure it directly. The next section proposes methodology to do exactly that.

The Link Structure of Online Political Communities

In this chapter, I survey the portions of the Internet that the average user is most likely to see while searching for common types of political information. I explicitly do not attempt to map every political site online or even every political site in a given category. The aim is not to overcome the limits imposed by the scale of the Web; rather, it is to demonstrate the biases these limitations introduce in the number and types of sites encountered by typical users.

The research design my colleagues and I have chosen comes out of a large body of established computer science research. (Part of that research is summarized in the appendix at the end of the book.) The methodology we implement has four main parts:

1. Create twelve lists of two hundred highly ranked "seed sites" in a variety of political categories. Six categories are chosen; in each category, one list is taken from Google search engine results, and one is taken from the Yahoo! directory service.
2. Build Web robots to crawl outward from these two hundred sites, following every link in turn, three links deep. For each crawl, this requires downloading roughly 250,000 HTML pages, or about 3,000,000 pages across all twelve crawls.
3. Classify these downloaded pages using Support Vector Machine (SVM) algorithms, to see whether newly encountered pages are relevant to the given category—if, for example, a page discovered by crawling away from gun control sites also focuses on gun control. Those pages that do belong in a particular category are classified as "positive."
4. For each of the twelve crawls, analyze the distribution of inlinks within the set of positive sites.

Ultimately, six categories of Web sites were chosen: sites on abortion, gun control, the death penalty, the U.S. Congress, the U.S. presidency, and the catchall category of "general politics." It is clearly infeasible to classify the downloaded Web pages with human coders. Even if one could classify 120 Web sites an hour, it would take an individual working eight hours per day ten years to classify three million pages. Human categorization also raises questions of bias and subjectivity.

To solve this problem, we classify these Web sites automatically using SVMs. The technical operation of SVMs are described in the appendix. The SVM classifier produces a reliable categorization of relevant Web pages. Most important, human coding (discussed below) suggests that it produces few false positives.

The choice of seed sites is obviously a critical one. Not only does this set of sites determine the starting point for the Web crawlers, and thus the area of the Web downloaded and analyzed, these sites are also used to train the SVMs to recognize relevant content. We were initially concerned about possible biases between human-categorized content and the machine-categorized content returned by search engines. Therefore, in each category, we analyze both seed sets generated by Google and seed sets taken from the human-categorized Yahoo! directory. Ultimately, both the Google and Yahoo! seed sets lead to the same conclusions.

Results

The six political topics examined are quite different from one another, and our research design introduces many sources of potential heterogeneity. The level of consistency in our results is therefore all the more striking. All twelve of the crawls reveal communities of Web sites with similar organizing principles and similar distributions of inbound hyperlinks.

First, let us examine the scope of the project. Table 3.1 lists the number of pages downloaded as well as the results of the SVM classification. The size of the crawls is quite large, averaging about a quarter of a million pages. The size of the SVM positive sets varies by subject; communities focused on particular political issues were smaller than those that focused on the presidency or the U.S. Congress. Out of the large number of pages crawled, only a fraction were relevant to the given category.

Table 3.1 suggests that the SVM classifier is good but not perfect. Human coding of five hundred randomly drawn positive Web sites found only nine where the human coder classified the Web page as unrelated to the issue area. Similarly, few sites in the negative set seem to be misclassified.[6] A significant portion of sites, however, are close to the SVM's decision boundary and are thus classified as "unsure." Sites about which

---

[6] Human coding of two hundred negative sites found no examples where the human coder disagreed with the SVM. This finding, however, may say less about the accuracy of the SVM classifiers than about the narrow diameter of the Web; for example, Reka Albert, Hawoong Jeong, and Barabási (1999) found that two random pages on the Web are, on average, nineteen clicks apart. This means that any large-scale crawl will quickly encounter lots of irrelevant content, and that even a classifier that put 100 percent of sites into the negative category would be right the large majority of the time.

Table 3.1
Number of Pages Downloaded and Results of SVM Classification

	Downloaded	Topical (SVM)	SVM unsure
Abortion (Yahoo!)	222,987	10,219	717
Abortion (Google)	249,987	11,733	1,509
Death penalty (Yahoo!)	212,365	10,236	1,572
Death penalty (Google)	236,401	10,890	938
Gun control (Yahoo!)	224,139	12,719	1,798
Gun control (Google)	236,921	13,996	1,457
President (Yahoo!)	234,339	21,936	2,714
President (Google)	272,447	16,626	3,470
U.S. Congress (Yahoo!)	215,159	17,281	2,426
U.S. Congress (Google)	271,014	21,984	4,083
General politics (Yahoo!)	239,963	5,531	1,481
General politics (Google)	341,006	39,971	10,693

This table illustrates the size of the Web graph crawled in the course of our analysis as well as the number of sites that the SVM classifiers categorized as positive. The first column gives the number of Web pages downloaded. Columns two and three give the number of pages that are classified by the SVM as having content closely related to the seed pages as well as the pages about which the SVM was hesitant.

the SVM was hesitant range from 7 to 25 percent of the size of the positive set. Human coding suggests that the large majority of these sites should be included in the positive set. Secondary analysis conducted with unsure sites included in the positive set found no substantive differences from the results detailed below.

In several cases, the Google and Yahoo! seed sets were quite different. There was initially some concern that the communities identified might not be directly comparable. Table 3.2, which shows substantial overlap between the positive sets from the different Yahoo! and Google crawls, does much to alleviate those fears. It suggests that the Yahoo! and Google crawls are exploring the same communities, and provides a clear demonstration of the small diameter of the Web. Most of the pages in the positive set are obscure and receive only a few inlinks. The least overlap occurs with pages with one hyperlink path to them. Among the most heavily linked pages, the overlap between the Yahoo! and Google results is almost complete.

The collection of Web pages found using these methods is between ten thousand and twenty-two thousand for all but one of the areas studied (table 3.2). Given the vastness of the Web, these pages are likely only a

Table 3.2
Overlap between Positive Sets from Yahoo! and Google Crawls

	Yahoo!	Google	Overlap
Abortion	10,219	11,733	2,784
Death penalty	10,236	10,890	3,151
Gun control	12,719	13,996	2,344
President	21,936	16,626	3,332
U.S. Congress	17,281	21,984	3,852
General politics	5,531	39,971	1,816

This table gives the overlap, on a given political topic, between the crawls generated by the Yahoo! seed set and those generated with the first two hundred Google results. The global overlap is significant, and a closer examination of the data suggests that overlap is nearly complete for the most heavily linked pages in each category.

Table 3.3
Links to Sites in the SVM Positive Set

	SVM positive set	Links to SVM set	Within-set links
Abortion (Yahoo!)	10,219	153,375	121,232
Abortion (Google)	11,733	391,894	272,403
Death penalty (Yahoo!)	10,236	431,244	199,507
Death penalty (Google)	10,890	291,409	149,045
Gun control (Yahoo!)	12,719	274,715	178,310
Gun control (Google)	13,996	599,960	356,740
President (Yahoo!)	21,936	1,152,083	877,956
President (Google)	16,626	816,858	409,930
U.S. Congress (Yahoo!)	17,281	365,578	310,485
U.S. Congress (Google)	21,984	751,306	380,907
General politics (Yahoo!)	5,531	320,526	88,006
General politics (Google)	39,971	1,646,296	848,636

This table gives the number of links to sites in the SVM positive set, from both outside the set and from one positive page to another. Note that in most cases, links from other positive pages provide the majority of the links.

small fraction of all pages on these topics. Of even greater interest than the size of these topical communities, though, is the way in which they are organized. Table 3.3 gives an overview of the link structure leading to these relevant pages.

Globally, the Web graph is sparse; a randomly selected series of pages will have few links in common. In contrast, the number of links between our

Table 3.4
Concentration of Links to the Most Popular Sites

	Sites	Links to top site (%)	Links to top 10 (%)	Links to top 50 (%)
Abortion (Yahoo!)	706	15.4	43.2	79.5
Abortion (Google)	1,015	31.1	70.6	88.8
Death penalty (Yahoo!)	725	13.9	63.5	94.1
Death penalty (Google)	781	15.9	53.5	88.5
Gun control (Yahoo!)	1,059	28.7	66.7	88.1
Gun control (Google)	630	39.2	76.8	95.9
President (Yahoo!)	1,163	53.0	83.2	94.9
President (Google)	1,070	21.9	65.3	90.9
U.S. Congress (Yahoo!)	528	25.9	74.3	94.8
U.S. Congress (Google)	1,350	22.0	51.4	82.3
General politics (Yahoo!)	1,027	6.5	36.4	70.3
General politics (Google)	3,243	13.0	44.0	74.0

This table demonstrates the remarkable concentration of links that the most popular sites enjoy in each of the communities explored. The first column lists the number of sites that contain at least one positive page; note that many sites contain numerous relevant pages. Columns two, three, and four show the percentage of inlinks attached to the top site, the top ten sites, and the top fifty sites in a given category.

positive pages is uniformly large. For ten of the twelve crawls, links from one positive page to another account for more than half the total. This increases our confidence that we have identified coherent communities of pages.[7]

Ultimately, what we want to know is the distribution of these inbound links. The first column of table 3.4 contains the number of *sites* in each category that contain at least one positive *page*. For example, Abortion-Facts.com is a prominent antiabortion Web site that contains within it many Web pages relevant to the abortion debate. If what we are interested in is the number of sources of political information, it makes greater sense

[7] It is worth noting that the results shown are based on raw data, and may thus inflate somewhat the connectedness of the graph. To take one example: MoratoriumCampaign.org, a popular site opposed to the death penalty, contains a number of heavily cross-linked relevant pages—and relevant page *A* may even contain more than one link to relevant page *B*. Eliminating cross-links between pages hosted on the same site eliminates a large portion of the links. The distribution of inlinks, however, remains stubbornly power-law distributed. Because we believe that the total number of inlinks is the best predictor of a site's visibility and traffic (Ding et al. 2002, Tomlin 2003), this analysis focuses on the raw numbers.

to count all of the pages at AbortionFacts.com as a single unit. The number of sites offering political information must, by definition, be smaller than the total number of pages.

The most important results are captured in the other three columns of table 3.4. Here we find the percentage of inlinks attached to the top site, the top ten sites, and the top fifty sites in each crawl. The overall picture shows a startling concentration of attention on a handful of hypersuccessful sites. Excluding one low-end outlier, the most successful sites in these crawls receive between 14 and 54 percent of the total links—all to a single source of information.

Particularly telling is the third column, which shows the percentage of inlinks attached to the top ten sites for each crawl. In nine of the twelve cases, the top ten sites account for more than half of the total links. The top fifty sites account for 3 to 10 percent of the total sites in their respective categories, but in every case they account for the vast majority of inbound links.

There is thus good reason to believe that communities of political sites on the Web function as winners-take-all networks. But is the inlink distribution among these sites governed by a power law? The answer seems to be yes. Consider the figures below: figure 3.1 looks at sites on the U.S. presidency, and figure 3.2 looks at sites devoted to the death penalty. One is generated from a Yahoo! seed set, and the other is from a Google seed set.

The unmistakable signature of a power-law distribution is that on a chart where both of the axes are on a logarithmic scale, the data should form a straight line. This is precisely what figure 3.1 shows: a textbook power-law distribution. A similar but less exact pattern is evident in figure 3.2, which is more typical of the communities crawled. Here, the line formed by the data on the log-log scale bulges outward slightly; the slope of the line gets steeper as the number of sites increases. The death penalty community deviates from a power law at the tails—particularly among the most popular sites, where a pure power law would produce astronomical numbers of links.[8]

Table 3.5 shows the results of fitting a power law to the data gathered by each of the twelve crawls. In this case, the model chosen is a simple

---

[8] The slightly curvilinear shape—which forms a soft, downward-facing parabola in the log-log scale—may suggest an admixture between a power law and some other distribution with an extreme skew (such as a log-normal distribution with a mean of 0).

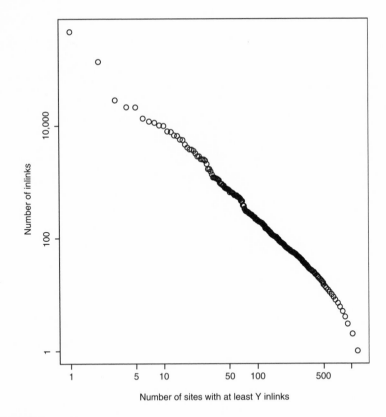

Figure 3.1
This chart shows the distribution of inbound hyperlinks for sites that focus on the U.S. presidency. Both axes are on a log scale. Note that the data form a straight line—unmistakable evidence of a power-law distribution.

ordinary least squares regression. The dependent variable is the log of the number of links pointing to a given Web site. For example, if site Q has 1,500 inlinks, its value on the dependent variable is equal to $ln(1,500)$, or 7.31. The explanatory variable is the log of the number of sites that have at least as many inlinks as site Q. Since a power-law relationship between the two variables should produce a straight line on a log-log scale, a linear regression on the log-transformed data is a straightforward way of testing how well such a distribution fits the data. In this context, the constant is the log of the number of inlinks that the model predicts for the community's most popular Web site.

This analysis shows that with a few caveats, a power law fits the distribution of inlinks within these political communities well. The Yahoo!

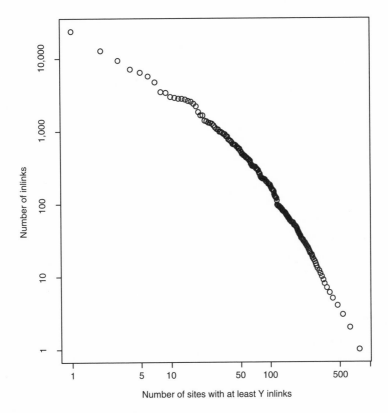

Figure 3.2
This figure illustrates the distribution of inlinks for sites focusing on the death penalty. Here again we see strong evidence of a power-law distribution, although there is a slight upward bulge to the plotted data. Fitting a power law to these data produces an R^2 of 0.952—the second lowest among the communities explored.

abortion community is a markedly poorer fit than the other eleven communities explored, though the power-law model still produces an R^2 of 0.902. The power-law model consistently predicts greater numbers of inlinks for the four or five most successful sites than we see in the data; to a lesser degree it underpredicts the number of sites that have only a handful of links. These deviations, particularly in the upper part of the curve, are substantively significant, as they dilute the concentration of attention on the small number of successful sites.

Still, even with outliers at both tails, power-law models produce an R^2 greater than 0.95 in eleven of the twelve communities. The body of the data, in *every* community, adheres strongly to a power law, and omitting

Table 3.5
Results of Fitting a Power Law to Crawl Data

	Coefficient $(-\alpha)$	Constant	R^2
Abortion (Yahoo!)	−1.544	11.834	.902
Abortion (Google)	−1.488	11.819	.972
Death penalty (Yahoo!)	−1.684	12.007	.977
Death penalty (Google)	−1.958	13.960	.952
Gun control (Yahoo!)	−1.458	11.650	.961
Gun control (Google)	−1.806	13.113	.968
President (Yahoo!)	−1.659	13.014	.992
President (Google)	−1.705	13.285	.975
U.S. Congress (Yahoo!)	−1.909	13.239	.971
U.S. Congress (Google)	−1.530	12.952	.953
General politics (Yahoo!)	−1.252	10.583	.956
General politics (Google)	−1.454	13.536	.977

This table shows the results of fitting a power law to the twelve communities explored, by means of an ordinary least squares regression on the logged data. The dependent variable is the log of the number of inlinks that a given site (e.g., site Q) has received; the explanatory variable is the log of the number of sites in the sample that have at least as many inlinks as site Q. If a power law follows the form $K^{-\alpha}$, the coefficent above is equal to $-\alpha$, the slope of the power-law line on a log-log scale. The constant represents the log of the number of links that the most popular site is predicted to receive.

the five highest and lowest link values usually produces a near-perfect fit. Inlink distribution within political communities is bound by powerful statistical regularities.

Site Visibility and the Emergence of Googlearchy

Whether online communities are better characterized by power laws or some other variety of extremely skewed distribution is, of course, not the central point. For political scientists concerned about the level of concentration within communities dedicated to political expression, two lessons are clear. First, the number of highly visible sites is small by any measure. It seems a general property of political communities online that a handful of sites at the top of the distribution receive more links than the rest of the relevant sites put together. Second, comparative visibility drops off in a rapid and highly regular fashion once one moves outside the core group of successful sites. The falloff in site visibility is not linear; rather, it follows an exponential function over many orders of magnitude. Given the diversity both in seed sets and the types of communities explored, these results are surprisingly strong and consistent.

One more point deserves emphasis: the power-law structure persists even if these sites are broken down into subcommunities. In the two crawls of the abortion community, for example, proabortion sites outnumber antiabortion sites by roughly three to one. Both anti- and proabortion sites are governed by a power law, however. Although the slope is different across the two groups (with antiabortion sites being more concentrated), the overall structure continues to focus attention on a few top sites. The same pattern is evident in the gun control and death penalty communities, which both contain clearly opposing subgroups. The structure of political groups on the Web thus may be considered fractal in nature—subparts of the community mirror the winners-take-all structure of the whole. Here again, political content reproduces results seen in other areas of the Web (Song, Havlin, and Makse 2005; Dill et al. 2002).

Taken together, the insights in this chapter add up to a new theory that my collaborators and I call Googlearchy: the rule of the most heavily linked. Building on previous research and the data referenced above, this theory offers several claims.

First, Googlearchy suggests that the number of links pointing to a site is the most important determinant of site visibility. Sites with lots of inbound links should be easy to find; sites with few inlinks should require more time and more skill to discover. All else being equal, sites with more links should receive more traffic.

Second, Googlearchy indicates that niche dominance should be a general rule of online life. For every clearly defined group of Web sites, a small portion of the group should receive most of the links and most of the traffic. Communities, subcommunities, and sub-subcommunities may differ in their levels of concentration; yet overall, online communities should display a Russian-nesting-doll structure, dominated at every level by winners-take-all patterns.

Third, Googlearchy suggests that this dependence on links should make niche dominance self-perpetuating. Heavily linked sites should continue to attract more links, more eyeballs, and more resources with which to improve the site content, while sites with few links remain ignored.

Since this original research was performed, other scholars have attempted to test whether search engines do reinforce the inequalities in link structure and traffic. Some scholars have presented data that search engines *are* worsening the rich-get-richer phenomenon, making online traffic more concentrated than would be produced by random surfing alone (Cho and Roy 2004). Others have disputed this claim, arguing that search engines make online traffic less concentrated than it would be otherwise (Fortunato et al. 2006).

The evolving debate over whether search engines produce a "vicious cycle" is important, but it should not obscure the larger point. The scholarly dispute focuses on how much online concentration can be blamed on search engines—and whether modern search methods are making inequality marginally better or worse. None of this research has disputed the conclusion that profound inequalities in links define search engine visibility and patterns of traffic.

The Politics of Winners-Take-All

The body of this chapter has focused on technical subjects of a sort that scholars of politics have rarely considered. It has talked about why link density is an effective proxy for online audience share. It has shown that communities of Web sites on different political topics are each dominated by a small set of highly successful sites. In concluding, we should remind ourselves why this matters. We know that the Web gives citizens millions of choices about where to go to get their political information. What we *have not* known, however, is how much the Web expands the number of choices that people actually use.

This lack of data has allowed scholars and public figures to make very different assumptions about the political impact of the Web. This chapter—and the three that follow—provide little support for the notion that the Internet is enabling an epochal shift from broadcasting to narrowcasting. Yes, almost anyone can put up a political Web site, but this fact matters little if few political sites receive many visitors. In the areas this chapter examines, putting up a political Web site is usually equivalent to hosting a talk show on public access television at 3:30 in the morning.

The scale of online concentration is so profound that it forces us to rethink not just the enthusiasm surrounding the Internet but also popular reasons for skepticism. Large sites are clearly important on the Web—Yahoo! dominates other portal sites, Amazon.com dominates online bookselling, eBay dominates online auctions, and online news is dominated by familiar names like CNN and the *New York Times*. What scholars have *not* generally understood, though, is that these winners-take-all patterns are repeated *on every level* of the Web.

The pervasiveness of these phenomena belies the explanations that political scientists have offered for them. We do not blame the high rate of functional illiteracy in the United States for Amazon.com's market dominance; it thus begs credulity to think that civic shortcomings are driving concentration in the political news market. The online political advocacy communities we studied in this chapter are not driven by commercial pressure, and yet the winners-take-all patterns within them are stark. Nor can we blame these patterns on powerful interest groups. The increasingly influential blog community began noncommercially and initially had little association with traditional political groups. And yet, as we shall see in chapter 6, blogs almost immediately replicated the winners-take-all distribution of links and traffic that we see in the Web as a whole.

The clear implication is that more fundamental forces are at work—and political scientists need to understand these larger phenomena before grafting traditional models of politics onto the online environment.

The theory of Googlearchy suggests that online concentration comes from the sheer size of the medium and the inability of any citizen, no matter how sophisticated and civic-minded, to cover it all. In many areas of political science, it is common to assume that most citizens know little about politics and take drastic shortcuts in the processing of political information. But if strong heuristics are needed to decide between two candidates on a ballot, how much more extreme do these heuristics need to be in deciding among millions of political Web sites? Previous scholarship has not emphasized enough this profound mismatch between the vastness of online political information and citizens' limited cognitive resources. Political scientists need more explicit models of how citizens respond to the astonishing overabundance of online information.

Scholars also need to reassess how the political possibilities of the Web are constrained by its architecture. The end-to-end design of the Web might not limit the political sites that citizens visit, but the link structure of the Web certainly does. If we want to gauge the ability of the Internet to amplify the voices of average citizens, we must first understand the patterns of concentration that govern online life—and online politics—even on the smallest scale.

Four

Political Traffic and the Politics of Search

As long as we're 80 percent as good as our competitors, that's good enough. Our users don't really care about search.
—Anonymous Web portal CEO, 1998, quoted in Google's corporate history

The previous chapter discussed the link structure of political sites on the World Wide Web. Link structure can provide a microscopic view of Web content, allowing us to survey the haves and have-nots within even the tiniest of online niches. If we take seriously claims that the Internet is a narrowcasting medium, this sort of method for small-scale analysis is indispensable. Still, the patterns seen in political communities in chapter 3 raise as many questions as they answer. To understand the Web's political impact, we need not just a microscope but also a big picture view of traffic on the Web. We need to put the winners-take-all patterns found within these small communities of Web sites into proper context.

To gauge the Internet's larger effects on the U.S. political landscape, then, we need to return to the sorts of questions that motivated the discussion in the preceding chapter, but this time on a broader scale. Where do people go online? How many visits do politically relevant Web sites receive against the broad backdrop of Web traffic? What sorts of citizens visit political sites? And where does traffic to political Web sites come from, anyway?

It may seem surprising that such fundamental questions have remained unanswered, but getting data on these subjects has been difficult. The decentralized nature of the Internet means that only large Internet service providers and dedicated Internet-tracking firms have access to representative data on online traffic patterns. This chapter was made possible through the assistance of Hitwise Competitive Intelligence, a firm that partners with large Internet service providers to collect and analyze Internet traffic. Hitwise provides subscribers only with anonymized, aggregate data, but the scope of the traffic that Hitwise analyzes is vast. As of May 2006, the Hitwise sample included data on 1,076,817 English-language Web sites.[1] Hitwise tracked traffic to these sites from ten million U.S. households that subscribed to its Internet service provider partners. Because (as we shall see) political Web sites account for only a tiny portion of overall Web traffic, the large Hitwise data set is preferable to data collected by other organizations, all of whom rely on far smaller samples.

Crucially, Hitwise provides clickstream data, allowing us to see—at least in the aggregate—which sites users visit before and after a particular Web site. This chapter thus examines not just the total traffic that accrues to each site but the paths that typical users take to get there.

As expected, Hitwise's clickstream data emphasize the role of search engines in directing traffic to politically relevant sites. One in five visits to news and media Web sites—and more than a quarter of the visits to political Web sites—comes directly from search engine queries. The last half of this chapter looks closely at the real-world queries that drive traffic to news sites and political advocacy sites. If search engines prove important in directing political traffic, the Hitwise data show that the way citizens use these tools is partly surprising.

Traffic data and query data both inform debates about the role of online gatekeepers. Whether sites like Google and Yahoo! should be seen as strong gatekeepers, or mere reflections of broader "democratic" social forces, has been the source of much dispute. Market concentration among search engine providers has been a particular source of concern, and three companies—Google, Microsoft, and Yahoo!—now handle 95 percent of all search engine queries (Tancer 2006). There have even been calls to regulate Google as a public utility (see, for example, Thierer and Crews 2003).

Would a more diverse search engine market provide more diversity in what citizens see? If the arguments for Googlearchy presented in the

---

[1] The number of Web sites that are included in Hitwise's traffic numbers varies over time. Sites are only ranked if they reach a minimum threshold of traffic; this means that Hitwise's monthly data always track a greater number of Web sites than the weekly data. Hitwise constantly updates its database to add new Web sites, and it performs regular audits to remove outdated entries.

previous chapter are correct, there should be substantial overlap between Yahoo!'s search results and those provided by Google. The last part of this chapter puts that claim to the test.

The Big Picture

Of all the things that discussions about online politics have been lacking, the most glaring has been a sense of scale. Here the Hitwise data are particularly helpful. As of this writing, no other data source measures traffic from such a large sample of the U.S. public, to such a large portion of the Web. By cataloging traffic to hundreds of thousands of the most visited sites on the Web, the Hitwise data can provide a much-needed sense of perspective.

While the appendix talks at greater length about the strengths and limitations of the Hitwise data, a few points should be repeated here. Hitwise's primary measure of traffic is the number of "visits" a site receives. Following standard industry practice, a visit is defined as a request for a Web page or series of Web pages from a site, with no more than thirty minutes between clicks. In general, this measure emphasizes sites that are visited frequently, but not *too* frequently. An individual who browses through Google's results many times a day, never going more than twenty-nine minutes between clicks, would be recorded as a single visit. The number of visits a site receives is a better metric of its proportional importance in the public's media diet than alternative metrics such as "audience reach," which measures the portion of the online population that visits a site at least once within a given window of time.

Figure 4.1 demonstrates visually just how important news sites and political sites are—or are not—in comparison to other online content, using Hitwise traffic data from March 2007. The outer circle represents the total volume of Internet traffic. Within it, smaller circles show the amount of traffic that goes to specific categories of Web usage. The figure is to scale: the area of each circle is proportional to the amount of traffic each category receives.

Overall, about 10.5 percent of Web traffic goes to adult or pornographic Web sites. A slightly smaller portion (9.6 percent) goes to Webmail services such as Yahoo! Mail or Hotmail, 7.2 percent of traffic goes to search engines, while only 2.9 percent of Web traffic goes to news and

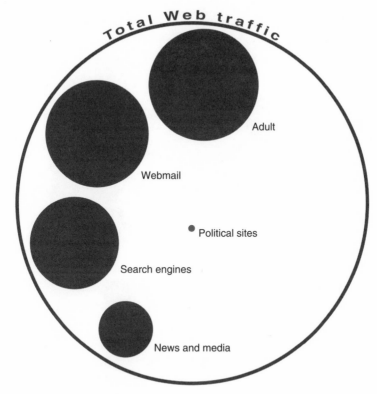

Figure 4.1
This figure displays the relative traffic received by different categories of online content. While adult sites receive more than 10 percent of Web visits, political sites receive slightly more than one-tenth of a percent.

media sites. These facts alone tell us much about citizens' priorities in cyberspace.

In the center of figure 4.1 is a small circle denoting the 0.12 percent of traffic that goes to political Web sites. This tally is so low that one might be tempted to assume that important sites have been omitted from the category. Yet (as subsequent graphics will show) a closer examination finds no obvious gaps in membership. The relative ranking of political sites within their niche matches our predictions; the community itself is just a far smaller slice of the Internet pie than many have imagined.

Figure 4.2 presents a more comprehensive picture of Internet traffic, at least at the top. Instead of looking at categories of content, this figure is a network map of traffic among the fifty most visited Web sites (with adult

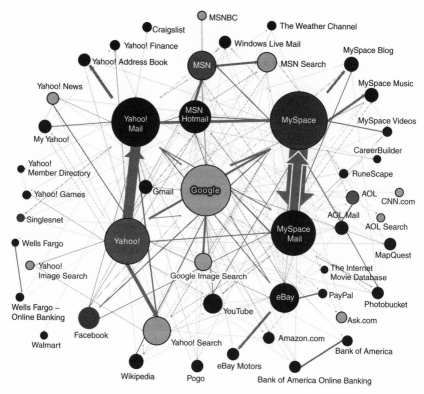

Figure 4.2
This figure maps traffic between the top fifty sites on the Web, according to Hitwise data from May 2007. Among other things, this graphic demonstrates the enormous disparity in traffic between the top ten Web sites and the other fifty.

sites omitted). As above, the traffic to a site is proportional to the Web site's area; the width of the lines between the sites is proportional to the number of users visiting site *A* immediately after site *B*. Because Hitwise has access to Internet service provider data, this does not necessarily mean that users followed a direct link between the two sites; they could also have used a browser bookmark or typed in a URL. The arrows indicate the direction of the traffic flow. To provide a sense of scale, MySpace, the most popular site in the figure, accounts for 6.3 percent of all nonadult Web traffic; Google attracts an additional 4.8 percent. The traffic between MySpace and MySpace Mail, the widest edge on the graph, represents 2.5 percent of all nonadult traffic.

Chapter 5 examines the issue of online concentration in detail and provides metrics that compare online concentration with that in traditional media. Yet it should be noted that this small set of sites gets a hugely disproportionate share of Web traffic. Taken together, these top fifty sites—out of the 773,000 that Hitwise tracked—received 41 percent of the Web traffic for the week of May 12, 2007, when these data were collected. Even this number is deceptive; there is an enormous disparity in traffic between the top seven or eight Web sites, and the rest of the top fifty. Every site listed gets a substantial portion of its traffic from at least one of the top ten Web sites. As expected, there is a great deal of traffic sharing between Google-, Yahoo!-, and MySpace-branded sites.

There are no political sites among this top fifty. If the graphic was expanded to include the top one hundred sites in the Hitwise data—or even the top five hundred sites—not a single political site would qualify for inclusion. For April 2007, HuffingtonPost.com and FreeRepublic.com were the most popular political Web sites. The Huffington Post ranked 796th among all nonadult Web sites, and Free Republic was ranked 871st.

Figure 4.3 performs a similar analysis, this time looking at traffic among the top fifty sites in Hitwise's news and media category. Hitwise describes the category as including "Web sites of magazines and newspapers, and news relating to the computer and IT industry"; Web sites for broadcasting corporations are also prominent members, including sites for the Weather Channel, CNN, MSNBC, and the BBC. Here again, the size of a site is proportional to the traffic it receives, and the edge width is proportional to the traffic flow.

The findings here are somewhat different from the findings for the Internet as a whole. The disparity between the largest and smallest sites is less extreme than in the previous map, and the largest sites play less of a role in directing traffic patterns. News sites are more a destination than a gateway to the rest of the Web; many of these sites get a substantial portion of their traffic from the top sites in the previous graph. In general, citizens do seem to get their online and off-line political messages from the same sources; even Web-only outlets, such as Yahoo! News, Google News, or the Drudge Report, rely almost exclusively on wire services and other traditional news organizations. Still, the online news market is not a perfect mirror of traditional media.

Given the magnitude of traffic flowing to other categories of online content, traffic to political sites is small enough to be a rounding error.

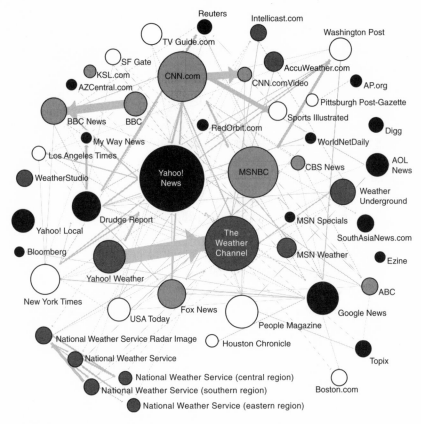

Figure 4.3
This graphic maps traffic among the top fifty sites in Hitwise's news and media category, as of May 12, 2007. Sites run by print outlets are in white, sites run by broadcast companies are in light gray, weather sites are in dark gray, and Web-only sites are in black.

As we have seen, some have hoped that this might be a blessing—that within sites focused on politics, traffic would be concentrated enough to highlight the best content, but diffuse enough to empower ordinary citizens.

Such hopes find little support in these data; the small volume of political traffic does not mean that the traffic is equitably distributed. Figure 4.4 maps the traffic among political Web sites. Hitwise defines political Web sites as those that "belong to particular political parties or organizations, plus sites that are devoted to expressing views on local or international

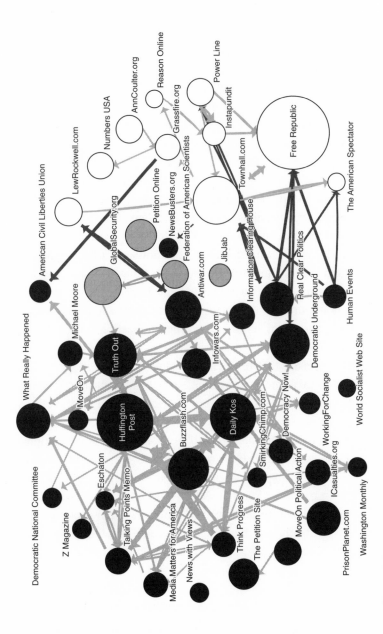

Figure 4.4

This figure maps traffic among the top fifty political Web sites, as of May 2006. Liberal- or Democratic-leaning sites are in black; conservative- or Republican-leaning sites are in gray; and self-declared neutral or nonpartisan sites are in gray.

political issues." Here the graph includes the top fifty political Web sites—a group that collectively receives 60 percent of the category's traffic. For political sites, we are concerned not just with the divide between the popular sites and the also-rans but also with the relative audience share among the most popular outlets. The most popular political sites listed include all of the expected names: online forums such as FreeRepublic.com, prominent advocacy groups such as MoveOn.org, and of course popular political blogs such as Daily Kos or Instapundit. Chapter 6 looks at blogs and blog rankings more closely; the ranking of top political blogs by traffic in Hitwise's account is nearly identical to the rankings of blogs based on either the number of inbound links they receive or other metrics of traffic.

Discussions of the online public sphere have imagined that political blogs, advocacy organizations, and other noncommercial outlets would challenge the monopoly that commercial media have had on public discourse. Judging by traffic, this challenge does not seem to be especially strong. News and media sites still receive thirty times as many visits as political Web sites do. That level of readership is large by the standards of traditional opinion journals, such as the *Nation*, the *New Republic*, or the *National Review*, all of which are minor print publications. Yet political sites remain a small niche amid the larger Web.

Chapter 2 suggested that liberals were more active Web users than conservatives, and this data is consistent with that conclusion. Overall, visits to liberal sites outpace visits to conservative sites by a margin of two to one.

Political sites do demonstrate strong liberal and conservative factions. In figure 4.4, political sites clearly share more traffic with their ideological compatriots, and these data provide some support for claims of online echo chambers (see, for example, Sunstein 2001). All told, only 2.6 percent of the traffic from one top fifty political Web site to another crosses ideological lines.[2] Still, twelve of the fifty sites receive or send a nontrivial portion of their traffic from across the aisle.

---

[2] Note that due to the limitations of Hitwise's data, only traffic sharing above a certain minimum threshold could be measured: in this case, traffic flows of at least 0.01 of a percent of all outgoing traffic from the community's most popular site (FreeRepublic.com during the month that these data were gathered). Any traffic sharing below this level of cross traffic was excluded from the analysis.

Table 4.1
Web Traffic by Household Income

	<$30k	$30–60K	$60–100K	$100–150K	$150K+
All Web sites	24%	28%	26%	14%	8%
News and media sites	23%	27%	26%	15%	8%
Political sites	23%	27%	30%	13%	6%

This table breaks down Web traffic by household income. Both news and media site visitors and political site visitors reproduce the income distribution of overall Web traffic.

Traffic Demographics

Hitwise also provides demographic data about visitors to these categories of Web sites. While the traffic information comes from Hitwise's Internet service provider partners, much of Hitwise's demographic information comes from pairing this traffic with an opt-in "mega panel" that includes a 2.5-million-subject subset of Hitwise's 10 million U.S. users. (Again, more details on Hitwise's methodology can be found in the appendix.) These opt-in panels—as with other forms of survey data—may be subject to some bias, as those who agree to participate may not be entirely representative of the broader online population. While Hitwise's opt-in panel methodology has been vetted by independent auditors, some details of how it works remain confidential. Still, Hitwise's panel data should do a good job of painting the broad strokes of traffic demographics in our areas of interest.

One curious thing about Hitwise's demographic data are what they do *not* show. Table 4.1 breaks down Web traffic by household income. The same three categories of Web use discussed above are represented here: all nonadult Web traffic, traffic to news and media sites, and traffic to political sites. These figures represent the percentage of site visits coming from households with these income levels.

In each case, the income disparities are modest. News and media site visitors and political site visitors show much the same income distribution as Web users as a whole.

For age and gender, however, the disparities in Web usage are dramatic (see table 4.2). Over the entire Web, Hitwise's sample shows that women account for slightly more Web traffic than men. Yet men generate substantially more of the traffic to news and political sites than women do. There is a 12 percentage point gender gap in online news traffic, and an

Table 4.2
Age and Gender of Web Site Visitors

	Male	18–24	25–34	35–44	45–54	55+
All Web sites	49%	20%	23%	23%	19%	16%
News and media sites	56%	12%	20%	22%	20%	26%
Political sites	59%	9%	13%	20%	25%	32%

This table shows the age and gender balance of site visitors for the four-week period preceding May 19, 2007. Men make up substantially more of the audience for news and politics than women do. The age disparities are even larger, with older Web users overrepresented in news and political traffic.

18 point male advantage in political site visits. Overall parity in online usage is not reflected in online news and politics.

Age differences in these data are also striking, and they provide a reality check on media reports that, over and over, have portrayed online politics as a youthful phenomenon. While general Internet use overrepresents younger citizens, online politics does not. Eighteen to thirty-four year olds account for 43 percent of all Web traffic, but they generate just 32 percent of the visits to news sites and only 22 percent of the visits to political sites. The converse is also true: while those forty-five and older are responsible for only 35 percent of general Web use, they produce 46 percent of the traffic to news and media sites along with 57 percent of the traffic to political sites. Nearly two decades of social science research has documented the decline of political engagement among the young (see, for example, Macedo et al. 2005). These data show that the Internet is not an easy solution to youthful disengagement.

Search Engines and (the Lack of) User Sophistication

Mapping broad patterns of online traffic, as we saw earlier in the chapter, emphasizes one unsurprising fact: much traffic on the Web is directed by search engines. Traffic to news and political sites is no exception. To understand how citizens reach politically relevant Web sites, then, we need to look more closely at the role that search engines play.

Recent research on search engines has stressed two central points. First of all, the large majority of the online population has used search engines. In early 2005, the Pew Internet and American Life Project found that 84 percent of Web users had used search engines at least once; on any given day, the study suggested, 56 percent of those online used a search engine to locate content (Fallows 2005). Search engine use has been widely adopted, but remains far from universal.

Second, most user interaction with these tools is unsophisticated. The Pew report's conclusion that users are "unaware and naive" mirrors other research, particularly digital divide scholarship that focuses on the skills and social support needed to use the Web effectively. Among these studies, some of the most systematic evidence comes from Eszter Hargittai's work with a large, representative sample of Internet users in a laboratory setting. Hargittai showed that many Internet users could not complete simple online tasks; asking subjects to find a political candidate's Web site was among the toughest challenges (Hargittai 2003).

This lack of user sophistication has specific implications for the types of searches that users employ. Many have reported that search phrases are typically short and highly general, with the large majority of searches employing only one or two terms (Silverstein et al. 1998; Jansen et al. 1998; Morahan-Martin 2004). Sophisticated search techniques—such as quotation marks, parentheses, and Boolean operators such as AND or OR— are employed in only a small portion of searches.

Second, this research emphasizes that the first page of results is particularly important. In one early study, Craig Silverstein and his colleagues analyzed roughly a billion queries—representing 285 million user sessions—contained in an AltaVista log file. The authors found that 85 percent of users did not look past the first page of results, and that users seldom modified their initial query (Silverstein et al. 1998; see also Spink et al. 2002; Jansen et al. 1998). Commercial usability studies and research on how users find health information have echoed these conclusions (Nielsen 1999; Morahan-Martin 2004). More recent studies have found that as search engines have improved, users have been viewing even fewer results pages (Jansen and Spink 2006).

AOL's August 2006 release of search data from 657,426 users reinforced this finding (Pass, Chowdhury, and Torgeson 2006). Consisting of randomly drawn user search sessions from March through May 2006, the AOL data showed that 90 percent of the total clicks went to sites on the first page of results. Even more striking, 74 percent of clicks went to the top five search results; the top result alone received 42 percent of all clicks.

These two themes are important in framing our understanding of search engines. Yet at the same time, this previous research also spotlights how much we have yet to learn. Placing users in a laboratory setting and assigning them to complete tasks may tell us what they are capable of, but it says little about what users seek out on their own initiative. Users may rely on short, general queries, but we still want to know *which* queries they use. What sorts of searches drive users to political Web sites?

The Hitwise data used in this chapter classify Web sites by category and subcategory. The *New York Times* Web site, for example, is included in both the News and Media category, and in the News and Media—Print subcategory. Classification is not exclusive. Traffic to the popular political blog DailyKos.com is included in both the Lifestyle—Blogs and Personal Web Sites and Lifestyle—Politics subcategories. Clickstream data allows Hitwise to record which search terms brought citizens to both individual Web sites and broader categories and subcategories of Web content.

For politics, we are especially interested in search traffic to two categories of Web sites. First, we want to understand the role that search engines play in directing citizens to news content. If there is indeed widespread citizen disinterest in politics, few of the queries that lead citizens to new sites should be political in nature. I examined the top 990 terms that citizens searched for immediately before visiting a news Web site. These data were collected in the first week of November 2005.

Second, and even more important, we want to know about the interaction between search engines and explicitly political Web sites. How much traffic do such Web sites get directly from search engines? What sorts of terms do citizens use when searching for politics? Do some types of search queries dominate? To answer these questions, I looked at the 1,020 most common searches that led users to political sites during the first week of November 2005.

What Users Search For

News-Related Queries

We begin by looking at news-related search queries. According to Hitwise, 19.5 percent of all news site visits came directly from search engines; an additional 16.5 percent of traffic came directly from portal front pages (such as Yahoo.com).

Table 4.3
Top Twenty Searches Leading Users to News and Media Web Sites

Rank	Query	% of total
1	weather	0.42%
2	hurricane wilma	0.26%
3	cnn	0.22%
4	news	0.15%
5	consumer reports	0.15%
6	janet jackson	0.13%
7	drudge report	0.13%
8	tv guide	0.13%
9	new york times	0.12%
10	myspace layouts	0.11%
11	bbc	0.11%
12	cnn.com	0.11%
13	martha stewart	0.10%
14	powerball	0.09%
15	usa today	0.09%
16	msnbc	0.09%
17	rosa parks	0.09%
18	drudge	0.08%
19	fox news	0.08%
20	bird flu	0.07%

This table shows the top twenty searches that led users to news and media Web sites during the week of November 7, 2005, according to data from Hitwise.

Table 4.3 presents the top twenty search queries that led users to news Web sites for the week of November 7, 2005. Several things are apparent from this list. We would expect that current events influence citizens' search terms, and this list supports that assumption. Many events from late October and early November 2005—such as the landfall of hurricane Wilma, the death of Rosa Parks, and concerns about bird flu—are reflected in this list.

Second, no single search term accounts for more than four-tenths of a percent of all news searches. This fact in itself is surprising. We saw highly concentrated patterns of links within communities of political Web sites in the previous chapter. In the first part of this chapter, too, we saw that broader patterns of traffic are an order of magnitude more concentrated than we see with these search queries.

These data suggest, then, that great diversity in search terms has not led to a similar diversity in traffic flow. Why? One reason is that two different search queries may lead citizens to the same source of information. Searches on Yahoo! or Google for "cnn," "cable news network," or simply "news" all return CNN.com as the top result. In the same vein, a few large sites such as Yahoo! or Wikipedia offer (literally) encyclopedic information on countless different topics. This hypothesis is consistent with evidence that the size of Web sites is power-law distributed; while a few sites have hundreds of thousands or even millions of pages, most sites have only a few pages of content (see, for example, Barabási and Albert 1999; Adamic and Huberman 2000).

Perhaps the most interesting findings come from a qualitative analysis of these queries. To better understand what citizens were searching for, each of the 990 news queries was further classified by human coders. The coders were asked to identify, first, whether the query seemed to be seeking a specific Web site, news organization, or information outlet. Searches for "drudge report," "tv guide," "yahoo news," or "cnn" were considered to be site-specific searches.

Second, the coders were asked if the query was political. If the search concerned a contemporary political issue or political news event, it was considered to be a political search. Searches for sites that focused principally on politics—as opposed to general news organizations or specialized outlets on nonpolitical topics—were also considered to be political searches.

The three individual coders made their coding decisions independently. The coding guidelines were designed to be highly inclusive about what classified as political content. Queries about general issues that had potential political dimensions—such as searches for "hurricane" or "vietnam"—were given the benefit of the doubt and classified as political. Despite an element of subjectivity, the agreement between any two coders was greater than 95 percent. Cases of coder disagreement were classified by majority rule.

Many scholars have concluded that a lack of skill limits citizens' online activities, and many queries did suggest a lack of user sophistication. As table 4.4 shows, the most popular search queries are short. Search engines process queries based on the number of terms they include, with

Table 4.4
Number of Search Terms in News and Political Queries

Terms	News	Politics
1	35%	26%
2	44%	43%
3	17%	19%
4	3%	7%
5+	<1%	6%

This table lists the number of terms in search queries that led users to news and media Web sites as well as political Web sites. The chart is based on November 2005 data from Hitwise.

spaces automatically used to separate terms—for example, "new york times" is a three-term query. Ninety-six percent of the news and media site queries in our sample used three or fewer terms.

Our sample of news searches included only a handful of misspellings; misspellings are, almost by definition, unlikely to end up on a list of the most common queries. Yet a surprisingly large number of the most popular queries were actually URLs, such as "cnn.com." Of the 990 queries, 119 of them—12 percent—included a .com or .org URL ending. Typing "cnn .com" into Google or Yahoo! will find the site, but such queries do suggest possible user confusion. There were also a number of popular search terms in which spaces were omitted, such as "usatoday," which indicate that users may be thinking of URLs.

The number of citizens searching directly for URLs is part of a broader finding. Most news searches in these data are *not* focused on current events or subjects of interest. A substantial majority of searches, rather, contain the names of specific news outlets or specific Web pages. Of the 990 total searches, 595—three-fifths—were searches for specific Web sites or online news outlets. In short, most searches involve citizens seeking out news organizations they are already familiar with.

Scholars have seldom provided clear and specific expectations about what citizens will choose to search for in the realm of politics and political news. Yet one common assumption is that citizens will begin with an interest in a political topic, and then type queries about that subject into search engines. Although much news traffic does come directly from search engines, news-related queries show a different pattern: citizens searching not for topics but for known sources.

This list of popular news-related queries is consistent with claims that few citizens are motivated to search out political information. Though coding was, if anything, overinclusive, only 69 of the 990 searches—7 percent—were classified as political. Weighting these queries by their popularity produces the same result, with political searches accounting for 7 percent of search traffic in the sample. Within these 69, 44—roughly three-fifths—were queries about political issues. Another 18—about one-quarter—were queries about political figures. Although the number of politically relevant news queries is too small to generalize from, it is safe to say that politically related queries are only a small portion of the searches that send citizens to news sites.

Political Searches

As we saw above, overtly political Web sites constitute a much smaller part of the online universe than do news Web sites—only 0.13 percent of nonadult Web traffic, or roughly 1 in 750 site visits. Search engines are more important in finding political content than they are for leading citizens to news sites. According to Hitwise, political Web sites as a category received 26.2 percent of their traffic directly from search engines in November 2005. This number, of course, does not include many surfers who may have originally found the site using a search engine but later return by using bookmarks, stored browser histories, or simply remembering the URL. It is easy to find sites where search engines account for even more of the traffic. In the previous chapter I mentioned AbortionFacts.com—the site that (as of this writing) has for several years been Google's top result for the query "abortion," and is currently Yahoo!'s number two result. According to Hitwise's December 2005 data, 80 percent of traffic to AbortionFacts.com came directly from search engines.

Proportionally, lower-traffic sites in this sample get more of their traffic from search engine referrals. For October 2005, the top 20 political Web sites averaged 18 percent of their visits from search engines. Sites ranked 101 through 120, by contrast, averaged 43 percent of visitors through search engine referrals.[3]

---

[3] A standard t-test shows the difference in means between these two groups to be highly significant, generating a t-value of 4.12.

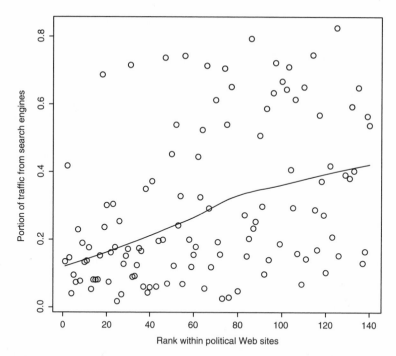

Figure 4.5
This figure plots the portion of traffic that political Web sites receive against their rank within the category. A LOWESS local regression line is overlaid on the data.

We can also show search engines' greater importance to small sites visually. Figure 4.5 plots the rank of sites within the politics category against the portion of visits they receive from search engine referrals. Despite the great variation in the traffic that individual sites receive, this graphic shows that less popular sites are, on average, more dependent on search traffic. A local regression line is overlaid on the graph, showing how the expected traffic from search engines grows as we move further down the ranking of political sites.

Political searches appear more concentrated than news searches, although the smaller number of political Web sites in our sample likely contributes to this finding. Hitwise tracked traffic to 518 popular political Web sites during the week studied. The 1,020 most popular search terms accounted for 19 percent of all the searches that led users to political Web sites. Table 4.5 presents the twenty most common searches. Human coding was used to sort these queries into five categories:

Table 4.5
Top Twenty Searches Leading to Political Web Sites

Rank	Search term	% of total
1	abortion	0.41%
2	jibjab	0.25%
3	michael moore	0.23%
4	vietnam war	0.21%
5	jib jab	0.21%
6	antiwar.com	0.20%
7	aclu	0.18%
8	ann coulter	0.18%
9	death penalty	0.14%
10	jibjab.com	0.14%
11	free republic	0.13%
12	infowars	0.13%
13	huffington post	0.13%
14	biodiesel	0.12%
15	failure	0.12%
16	huffington	0.11%
17	truthout.org	0.11%
18	huffingtonpost.com	0.11%
19	democracy now	0.11%
20	american spectator	0.11%

This table shows the top twenty searches that led users to political Web sites, according to November 7, 2005, data from Hitwise.

1. Queries about political issues
2. Queries naming specific Web sites or online outlets
3. Queries about political organizations
4. Queries about political personalities
5. Miscellaneous queries

The coding was exclusive, with every term placed in one of the five categories. When a query might conceivably belong in more than one category, preference was given to what seemed the primary intention of the user. A search for "Michael Moore," for example, was classified as a search for a political personality, while a search for "michaelmoore.com" was classified as a search for a specific site. Agreement between the coders was high; pairwise comparison among the three coders exceeded 90 percent in every case.

Here, of course, political search terms do not have to compete with queries seeking the weather report or television listings. The largest category consisted of queries about political issues. Just under half of the searches—487 of the 1,020—were classified as issue queries. Weighted by popularity, issue queries were proportionally less important, accounting for 39 percent of the referred traffic.

Just as with political news, a substantial number of political searches focus not on issues but on outlets. Fifteen percent of the searches—154 out of 1,020—were seeking specific Web sites. As the top twenty search terms suggest, though, this category of query was disproportionately popular, accounting for 27 percent of the search traffic in our sample. Here again many queries included URL information; forty-three searches included .com, and seventeen included .org.

In addition to those who searched for specific Web sites, 13 percent of the queries and about 12 percent of the referred traffic involved searches for specific political organizations. In most cases, the organization's official Web site was the first result on both Yahoo! and Google.

Another common theme in these queries were searches for political personalities. Typically consisting of just the first and last name of a public official or political figure, these 190 personality-focused searches amounted to 17 percent of the searches by traffic.

Lastly, 5 percent of the searches (fifty-four queries) fell into the miscellaneous category. This group included queries that did not fit cleanly into any other classification. The largest component of the miscellaneous category were "adult" or sexually explicit searches; twenty-five of the fifty-four miscellaneous queries fit this description. Only a few queries in this category had any obvious relationship to politics.

For political searches, then, just as with news-related searches, a substantial portion of users are seeking not topics of interest but familiar information outlets. Overall, roughly two-fifths of the queries by traffic were looking for either specific Web sites or specific organizations. These searches are naturally less likely to lead citizens to new information sources or divergent political perspectives.

Search Engine Agreement

These search query data highlight somewhat unexpected patterns in the search behavior of users. But ultimately, we want to know not just what citizens search for but the interaction between the chosen queries and the most popular search tools. The Googlearchy hypothesis predicts that there should be substantial overlap in the results provided by modern search engines. Of particular concern are Yahoo! and Google, which together handle more than four-fifths of all U.S. search queries (Tancer 2006). For political content, how much does it matter which search engine citizens use? Is search engine agreement higher for some sorts of queries than for others?

The simplest way to address these questions is to plug these 1,020 political queries into Yahoo! and Google, and calculate the level of agreement. To this end, a simple methodology was adopted. First, a small computer program (generously provided by Seaglex Software) was used to send each of these queries to Yahoo! and Google, and then to parse the HTML pages of Yahoo! and Google results. Because most searches do not go beyond the first page, only the first ten results (the default number included on Yahoo! or Google's first page) were analyzed. Sponsored links—such as targeted advertising, or links to internal Yahoo! or Google content—were ignored.

Second, a Perl script was used to compare agreement between the Yahoo! and Google results. For both theoretical and practical reasons, comparison was done at the level of the Web domain, not the specific Web page returned. Concerns about media diversity have focused on the number of media sources that citizens are exposed to, not the specific news articles or broadcast programs they see. In this context, the larger Web domain (such as NYTimes.com or NationalReview.com) most closely corresponds to traditional media outlets (such as the print versions of the *New York Times* or the *National Review*). Moreover, if Google's top result is www.example.com, and Yahoo!'s top result is www.example.com/index.htm, some page-based comparisons will miss the fact that both URLs resolve to the same Web page.[4]

---

[4] One key advantage of the Hitwise data is that Hitwise's technology is able to detect automatic redirection and identical site content, and is thus able to sidestep this problem.

Table 4.6
Agreement between Yahoo! and Google across Types of Political Queries

Category	% of traffic	Top result	Top five	Top ten
Political issues	39%	42%	61%	47%
Site specific	27%	100%	—	—
Political personalities	17%	66%	65%	46%
Political organizations	12%	90%	73%	55%
Miscellaneous	5%	37%	53%	41%

This table shows agreement between Yahoo! and Google for different categories of political queries.

Methods that compare the text of the URLs have additional limitations. In searches for "abortion," both Yahoo! and Google place the National Abortion Rights Action League (NARAL) near the top of their results. Yet the NARAL Web site uses two different URLs; Yahoo! knows the site as ProChoiceAmerica.org, while Google points users to NARAL.org. While some specific instances (including this one) were corrected by hand, text-based comparisons may thus understate the true level of agreement.

Nonetheless, this methodology can help us understand to what degree—and in what areas—the two most popular search engines agree with one another. Table 4.6 presents the results of this analysis. For each of the five categories, it shows Yahoo! and Google agreement for the top site, the top five sites, and the top ten sites.[5]

Which of these measures is most important likely depends on the specific category considered. For site-specific searches and searches about specific political organizations, citizens seem to be seeking a single online outlet. Agreement on the top site would therefore be the most critical metric. For searches containing the name of a specific political organization, Yahoo! and Google agree on the top result 90 percent of the time. For site-specific searches, the agreement between search engines is even higher. In every case—a full 100 percent of queries in the site-specific search category—Yahoo! and Google agreed on the top result. For queries that contained URL information (about one-third of this category), Google returned not the typical ten results but only a single result pointing to the

---

[5] The Yahoo! and Google results used for comparison were collected during the last week of November 2005; all searches within a given category (such as political issues or political personalities) were performed on the same day.

relevant URL. For this reason, it was not possible to compare Yahoo! and Google results in this category beyond the top site.[6]

For political personalities and political issues, the key metric is likely different. Here most users do not seem to be seeking a specific online outlet. For these categories, agreement among the top five results—the results a typical user can see without downward scrolling—would seem to be most important. Our methodology finds a 61 percent "top five" overlap between Yahoo! and Google for political issue searches, and a 65 percent agreement for searches focusing on political personalities.

Google and Yahoo! use different ranking algorithms and different methods of crawling the Web. Yet even in political issue searches—the area where the overlap is smallest—these data suggest that Google and Yahoo! will typically have three of their top five sites in common.

How Wide a Gate?

As this chapter shows, search engines do direct an enormous volume of Web traffic. Yet despite the importance of these tools, there has been much disagreement over the role that search engines play. Are search engines strong gatekeepers, with a great deal of autonomous influence in directing Web traffic? Or are search engines simply mediators, mirroring existing institutions and social structures?

To some degree, of course, the answer is "both." Public discussion of search engines' gatekeeping role has focused in part on the economic power of search providers. Certainly Google and Yahoo! have become large and successful companies; as of May 2007, Google's market capitalization was $151 billion, while Yahoo was valued at $38 billion. (The next chapter will look at the economics of these firms in more detail.)

Yet while market power matters, economics are not the whole story. The structure of the Web matters too. The substantial overlap between Yahoo and Google's search results seems to reflect winners-take-all linkage patterns. Users' reliance on short, general queries, and their overall lack of sophistication, also truncates the content seen by the public. As of March 2006, Google claimed to find 837,000,000 results for a query on

---

[6] Since this research was performed, Google has changed this policy; entering a site URL into Google now returns a full results page.

"politics," a remarkable technological feat; yet this huge aggregation of content matters little if few users venture past the first page of search results—or even scroll down to the bottom of that first page.

Citizens do seem to be finding what they seek online. In addition to the fact that most searches do not venture past the first page of results, most users express confidence in their ability to find what they are looking for (Fallows 2005). Still, those who had hoped that the Internet would expand the political information citizens access have to contend with two central facts. First, relatively little of what citizens are looking for is political. Search engines, along with Web portals, are major conduits of traffic to news Web sites. But citizens are more likely to get the weather report and the sports scores online than to follow political issues.

Second, much of what citizens seek is familiar. Roughly three-fifths of searches for news are source specific; about 40 percent of political searches are similarly seeking specific sites or specific political organizations. Queries focused on familiar organizations and outlets are less likely to expand the sources of political information that citizens use.

This is another way, then, that search engines help keep the attention of the public highly centralized. Yahoo! and Google allow citizens to find new Web sites, but they also make it easy for users to return to known sources. The Web may have allowed millions of small-scale Web sites to proliferate; yet for news and politics, these smaller sites are usually not what citizens are seeking.

For politics, debates about search engines should not be allowed to distract us from more fundamental concerns. Against the broad backdrop of online traffic, news and political sites are of secondary importance. Only about three of every hundred site visits is to a news and media Web site. Slightly more than one site visit in a thousand is to a political Web site. Pornographic content is two orders of magnitude more popular than political content.

The patterns of online traffic detailed in this chapter should help weaken many persistent myths about online political discourse. Web sites for political advocacy and even prominent political blogs get only a tiny fraction of the attention that traditional news outlets receive. Older citizens far outpace younger ones in visits to political Web sites.

Still, the biggest and most consistent problem with debates about online politics has been an absence of perspective. Scholars, public officials, and journalists have paid a great deal of attention to online politics. Citizens themselves, though, have directed their attention elsewhere.

Five

Online Concentration

What information consumes is rather obvious: it consumes
the attention of its recipients. Hence a wealth of information
creates a poverty of attention, and a need to allocate that
attention efficiently among the overabundance of
information sources that might consume it.

—Herbert A. Simon, *Computers, Communications,
and the Public Interest*, 1971

From law to public policy, democratic theory to party politics, interest in
the Internet has begun from the belief that the Web is democratizing the
flow of information. Chapters 3 and 4 have looked at patterns of online
attention at both the macro- and microlevels. This chapter goes further,
directly challenging the notion that Web audiences are less concentrated
than those for traditional media. If true, this fact alone should shift our
expectation about who gets heard online.

This claim—that audiences are as concentrated online as off-line—
will be controversial, and in part the previous two chapters have been
intended to lay the foundation for it. They have suggested many potential
reasons for this concentration. For average citizens, or even for super-
human ones, navigating billions of Web pages requires drastic cognitive
shortcuts. Power-law patterns in the link structure of the Web channel
users toward heavily linked sites. Most citizens do not venture beyond the
first page of search results, many use search tools to find familiar sources,
and search engines themselves often agree on which sites are most relevant. This chapter will add to this list, showing that the economic structure
of online content production also encourages audiences to cluster around a
small set of successful Web sites.

This chapter's central goal, however, is to measure just how concentrated online audiences are. The hope is that readers will find the
book's explanations persuasive, and that by the end they will view online

concentration as expected or even overdetermined. Yet for politics, it is important to measure the extent of online concentration no matter what gives rise to it. My questions here are straightforward: What portion of online readership accrues to the most popular outlets? How do the patterns we see online compare to those we have become accustomed to in traditional media? Claims about the Internet are comparative; its political effects are presumed to come from displacing mainstream media outlets. Is the Internet really a sharp break with the broadcast model?

Barriers to Entry

In order to understand concentration in new media, we need to begin by reviewing a few basic lessons about concentration in the old. Market concentration is one area where economists are in near-complete agreement. In the absence of a legal monopoly or predatory business practices, concentrated markets are those that allow economies of scale—that is, the more that a firm produces, the lower its average costs.

Consider the venerable newspaper, the oldest medium of mass communication. For the past several decades, fewer than 1 percent of U.S. daily newspapers have had a direct competitor in the same city (Dertouzos and Trautman 1990; Rosse 1980). Economics research has concluded that these local newspaper monopolies result from economies of scale; because the largest firm is able to operate at a lower average cost, it drives smaller competitors from the market (see, for example, Rosse 1967, 1970; Dertouzos and Trautman 1990; Reddaway 1963). Newspapers face high fixed costs and low marginal costs. Producing the first copy of a newspaper is extremely expensive, requiring a large staff and substantial infrastructure; producing a second copy costs only pocket change.

Newspapers and broadcast media in this regard have a similar cost structure to utilities such as water, telephone, or electricity—classic examples of "natural" monopolies. For water or electric service, a large initial investment in physical infrastructure is required. Wiring must run from the generating station to the household, and plumbing must run from a reservoir to the home and back to a wastewater treatment facility. Getting the first gallon of water to a home may require thousands of dollars, but the second, third, and thousandth ones cost little. Software is another oft-cited example of a natural monopoly: while developing a piece of software requires substantial developer effort, producing perfect copies of the finished product is cheap.

What I want to suggest is that many online markets similarly face high fixed costs and low marginal costs, and that widespread talk about how the Internet is "lowering barriers to entry" can thus be misleading. Many online market segments are hugely capital-intensive. First movers enjoy a substantial advantage. And because large up-front investments can be averaged over the entire user base, online markets often provide large economies of scale.[1]

I talked briefly in the last chapter about the economics of the search engine market. In fact, Yahoo! and Google are content providers, with search results a critical form of online content. For Google to become the market leader, the company needed more than just a bright idea for a new search algorithm. It also required massive capital investment, with hundreds of millions of dollars spent on research, personnel, marketing, and software code—not to mention the physical hardware necessary to handle billions of queries a day.

The company's financial statements starkly emphasize these facts. Since Google became a public corporation in August 2004, the company has disclosed far more of its finances. For the 2005 fiscal year, Google (2005, 40) reported $6.14 billion in revenues. Forty percent of that money went directly to "Costs of Revenues," primarily traffic acquisition costs—money paid to advertising partners and others who directed users to Google's sites. The traffic that Google receives is thus not just the natural result of having an attractive Web site; Google pays out billions of dollars annually to have other Web sites funnel visitors to its online properties. As of December 31, 2005, Google employed 2,093 people to do research and development; the company spent $484 million on research and development over the 2005 calendar year (Google 2005, 18, 41).

Perhaps the biggest surprise on Google's balance sheet has been the huge sums spent on capital equipment. For 2003 through 2005, the company reported a net income of $1.97 billion, but spent $1.33 billion on property and equipment. In other words, capital expenditures over this three-year period soaked up two-thirds of Google's net income. At the end

---

[1] In a similar vein, some scholars have seen the probable convergence of the Internet with television broadcasting as reinstituting high barriers to entry—and thus reducing content diversity (Gandy 2002; Owen 1999; Roscoe 1999). I argue here that barriers to entry have never been as low as these scholars contend.

of 2005, Google listed $949 million in information technology equipment as assets. One analyst called Google's capital equipment spending "unfathomably high," noting that Google spent the same portion of its revenue on equipment as a typical telephone company (Hansell 2006). Even so, Google CEO Eric Schmidt said that this spending was not enough. Referring to the enormous volume of Web pages, e-mail, and video on the company's servers, Schmidt declared that "those machines are full. We have a huge machine crisis" (quoted in Hansell 2006).

What has it taken for other search engines to compete with Google? Judging by Yahoo!'s and Microsoft's examples, the unsurprising answer is "lots of money." In many respects, Yahoo!'s finances look similar to Google's. Yahoo! reported $5.26 billion in revenues during fiscal 2005; yet as with Google, Costs of Revenues ate up 40 percent of Yahoo!'s revenue, with (again) most of that sum spent on acquiring traffic. In the same year, Yahoo! (2005, 66) spent $1.03 billion on marketing and $547 million on product development, a category that included improvements to its Web site and general research and development costs. As of December 2005, Yahoo! reported owning $838 million in computer equipment.

Yahoo! illustrates barriers to entry in the search engine market in another way as well. For most of its history, Yahoo! relied on other companies to provide search results for its Web portal. In the first quarter of 2004, Yahoo! stopped licensing search technology from Google and switched to its own, in-house search engine. Yahoo! bought its search technology through a rapid series of corporate acquisitions in 2003, ultimately absorbing Inktomi, Overture, and existing search engines such as AltaVista and All the Web. Inktomi cost Yahoo! $290 million; Overture cost a whopping $1.7 billion (Yahoo! 2005, 47).[2] As Yahoo! CEO Terry Semel described it, the financial costs and strategic risks of these deals were huge, yet Yahoo! feared that without these acquisitions it would be impossible to enter the search business. Said Semel (2006), "We bet everything we had—we bet the company on those acquisitions, because if it failed we would have been in serious problems, and if we had allowed one of the other guys to get it and shut us out, we would have been in [an] even greater situation."

Microsoft's search engine investment is harder to quantify based on the company's financial disclosures, but there is no doubt that it has been similarly

---

[2] Yahoo! acquired Overture shortly after it acquired AltaVista and All the Web.

enormous. In May 2006, Microsoft announced that it would spend $2 billion more than expected over the coming year. Microsoft claimed that this extra spending was needed to compete with Google (Lohr and Hansell 2006).

The same capital-intensive spending patterns visible with search engines can be seen in other online markets. Consider another prominent online business: Amazon.com. Amazon's original business model made it clear that the company would only be profitable at enormous sales volumes; the hope was that after building a large customer base and investing in extensive off-line and online infrastructure, few booksellers would be able to compete. Amazon bet that the Internet would produce *high* barriers to entry that would limit future competition. The wager seems to have been correct. The Amazon.com (2005) operation is now an enormous (and enormously expensive) one, with $8.14 billion in revenue for 2005. Amazon's nearest competitor, BarnesandNoble.com (2005, 30), had 2005 online sales of $440 million—5 percent of Amazon's online sales.

The difficulty of competing against an established online firm like Amazon.com can also be seen in the example of Borders.com. The Borders Group is a large national bookselling chain, with established distribution channels and a wide customer base. But after struggling to make its Web site profitable, Borders in August 2001 threw in the towel and agreed to let Amazon.com take over all of its Web site operations (Soto 2001). Any corner bookstore can put up a bare-bones Web site for a minimal investment. But if a company like Borders cannot play in the same league as Amazon.com, who can? How can Mom and Pop's Books compete effectively against a company that spent $451 million in 2005 just developing, maintaining, and improving its Web properties (Amazon.com 2005, 50)?

These financial data force us to reconsider the supposed differences between online and traditional markets. No one looks at telephone companies—or even software companies—and assumes that the barriers to entry are low. Yet this argument still remains common in online markets where firms face similar cost structures. The same financial pressures blamed for market concentration in the off-line world are quite visible online.

Distribution, Not Production

Blanket claims that the Internet is lowering the barriers to entry, then, are at odds with the evidence. Yet in one key area, the Internet is altering the cost structure of media firms and content producers: it lowers the cost of distribution. Consider the music industry. Distributing songs through online music services like Apple's iTunes saves the cost of pressing and distributing a compact disc, and the costs associated with maintaining a retail storefront. Even if all of their sales were online, however, record labels would still have to pay promotional costs, studio time, artist royalties, and a host of other expenses. One recent estimate suggests that eliminating the physical distribution of compact discs would save record labels only about 25 percent (Anderson 2004).

Returning to the example of newspapers is even more instructive. For newspapers, it is generally far cheaper to pay for a Web site than to pay for printing presses, press operators, paper, ink, delivery vans, and delivery people. Yet whether their readers are online or off-line, newspapers still have to pay reporters, editors, janitors, and office staff; they still require offices, desks, computers, and telephones. To understand how much the Internet matters, it makes sense to divide newspaper spending into two categories: the money spent creating articles, photographs, and other content; and the money spent printing and distributing that content. If all of the *New York Times'* readers suddenly switched to the online edition, printing costs would disappear, but the first category of costs would remain largely unchanged.[3]

Since many newspaper companies are public, they are required by law to disclose some of their internal finances. The accounting that the Securities and Exchange Commission requires is not perfect for our purposes but it does offer insight into how much newspapers spend to print and distribute their paper product. The New York Times Company, for instance, is one of the largest newspaper firms by circulation; it publishes the *New York Times*, the *Boston Globe*, the *International Herald Tribune*, and smaller regional papers like the *Worcester Telegram & Gazette*.

Newspapers are a labor-intensive industry. As the New York Times Company (2005, F4) explains in its annual report, "The News Media Group's main operating expenses are employee-related costs and raw materials, primarily newsprint." In 2005, the New York Times Company (2005) spent $321 million on raw materials, accounting for 11 percent of

---

[3] For example, Robert Picard (2002, 64) notes that newspapers would be eager to use the Internet to save on production and distribution costs, but that any savings would come only if the readership and advertising revenue remained constant—an unlikely assumption.

the collective operating expenses of its newspapers. Labor costs for the company are larger than raw material costs, at $691 million (New York Times 2005, F22).

While a breakdown of labor costs across the different news organizations under the Times Company's umbrella is difficult, for the *New York Times* itself the paper's labor agreements tell us much about how these employee-related costs are distributed. The large majority of the *Times'* workforce is unionized; roughly 3,000 *Times* employees are union members (New York Times 2005, 10).[4] The membership of these labor unions isolates "production employees"—typesetters, stereotypers, drivers, operating engineers, press operators, and so on—from those responsible for the paper's content. Sixteen hundred *Times* employees are members of the New York Newspaper Guild, which represents the paper's journalists, photographers, and editors. The remaining 1,400 unionized employees are members of production or delivery unions. More than half of the *Times'* unionized staff is thus devoted to content creation—the category of costs on which the Internet has little impact.

Another glimpse into newspaper finance comes from the Knight Ridder Corporation, which at the end of 2005 was the second-largest newspaper firm by circulation.[5] Knight Ridder owned thirty-two daily newspapers and sixty-five nondaily newspapers in twenty-nine markets. In the 2005 fiscal year, Knight Ridder (2005, 40) had total operating costs of $2.51 billion. Of this sum, Knight Ridder paid $413 million for newsprint, ink, and other consumables—16 percent of the company's total operating costs. Knight Ridder (2005, 21) listed production costs of approximately $130 million, and circulation costs of approximately $330 million. In short, printing and distribution were only about a third of Knight Ridder's operating costs.

---

[4] Overall, the New York Times Media Group has 4,800 full-time-equivalent employees. This group includes not just the *Times* itself, however, but also the radio station WQXR, the New York Times News Service, NYTimes.com, the *International Herald Tribune*, and the Discovery Times cable television channel. According to the annual report, the *International Herald Tribune* has 350 full-time employees; information is not provided on the number of employees for the other subdivisions. Note that management employees are also not included in the union rolls.

[5] In early 2006, unhappy Knight Ridder shareholders forced the sale of the company; it was purchased by the McClatchy Company, another newspaper chain, in June 2006. Knight Ridder's fate is a further illustration of the difficulties facing papers in smaller markets.

For news content, then, claims that the Internet will transform citizens from consumers to producers are problematic. For content that is intrinsically cheap to produce, lower distribution costs might matter. With political blogs, anyone with a minimum of computer savvy and an opinion can post their thoughts online; yet blogging is something of an exception. For content that is already expensive to create, but where average distribution costs are low, the Internet does not change the economic logic of concentration. If anything, the Internet's ultralow distribution costs would seem to guarantee even larger economies of scale.

In one big way, however, the Internet does change the rules for traditional media outlets. Geographic boundaries have long served to limit the competition that local media outlets face. While over-the-air broadcasting cannot be heard outside a station's region, local broadcasting outlets now have to contend with cable and satellite broadcasters. Historically, newspapers have benefited from geographic barriers even more than radio and television stations have. As Philip Meyer (1995, 40) describes it, for most of the twentieth century "a monopoly paper [was] a tollgate through which information passe[d] between the local retailers and their customers.... Owning the newspaper was like having the power to levy a sales tax." It is still the case that only three newspapers have significant national circulations: the *New York Times*, the *Wall Street Journal*, and *USA Today*. Yet online, local newspapers now compete with thousands of other outlets from around the country and the world. Many have blamed the Internet for recent declines in newspaper circulation; by fall 2006, three years of cumulative losses had eaten up 6.3 percent of daily circulation, and 8 percent of Sunday circulation (Project for Excellence in Journalism 2007). The decline in newspapers' employment and classified advertising has been particularly notable, as local papers now face competitive pressure from Web sites such as Craigslist and Monster.com.

These changes force us to ask, At which level are we to measure diversity? For individual citizens, the Internet has increased their choice of news outlets by several orders of magnitude. Residents of Walla Walla, Washington interested in international news no longer have to be content with the *Walla Walla Union-Bulletin*; they can read the *New York Times*, the *London Times*, or even the *Times of India*. Yet discussions about media diversity most often take place in the context of national politics. The common suggestion is that because of the Internet, Americans as a whole will rely on a

Table 5.1
Audience Share for Online and Off-line Media

	N	Top 10	Top 20	Top 50	Top 100	Top 500
All Web sites	1,325,850	26%	30%	35%	40%	51%
News and media	7,041	29%	37%	47%	56%	79%
Political sites	970	31%	43%	62%	77%	99%
Radio audience	1290	7%	11%	21%	33%	77%
Newspaper circulation	1058	19%	29%	46%	61%	91%
Magazine circulation	653	27%	36%	52%	67%	98%

This table presents data on audience share for both online and off-line media outlets. The Web data come from Hitwise Competitive Intelligence, the radio data are from the Arbitron corporation, and newspaper and magazine circulation comes from the Audit Bureau of Circulations.

broader set of news outlets and political information sources. At the national level, however, an increase in diversity is not a foregone conclusion.

Online Concentration

Before looking at concentration across media, we should begin by examining patterns of Web traffic on their own. Here again, the Hitwise data allow us to look at Web usage on both the macro-and microlevels. These data are not as fine grained as that in chapter 3; the crawling and classification techniques used there found more than one thousand sites with abortion-related content, for example, while Hitwise's *entire* politics category for May 2006 consisted of less than a thousand Web sites. At the same time, the Hitwise data allow us to look directly at audience share, rather than using indirect measures such as inbound links.

Table 5.1 illustrates the portion of audience captured by the top outlets for both online and off-line media. Set aside for a moment the lower three rows of this table, which deal with radio audiences and print circulation, and consider just the first three rows. The first row presents aggregate data for all 1.3 million Web sites that Hitwise tracked in February 2006. Below it are concentration figures for the more than 7,000 news and media Web sites, and the 970 political Web sites that Hitwise tracked over the same period.

Given the vast expanse of online content, it is startling how narrowly users focus on the top few Web sites. Hitwise categorizes Web sites conservatively, separating out (for example) visits to mail.yahoo.com from visits to the main Yahoo! Web portal. Despite this, the top ten sites receive more than one-quarter of all Web visits.

Yet the large market share of the most popular sites is not the whole story. While the top five sites receive 20 percent of all Web traffic, accounting for 50 percent of Web traffic requires us to look at the top five hundred sites. The lower end of the audience distribution is far more fragmented than that for traditional media. Individually, each of these lower-ranked sources is insignificant; yet collectively, these sites account for a substantial fraction of Web traffic.

Chapter 3 argued that the Web was fractally organized, with winners-take-all patterns at every level. The Hitwise data are consistent with this hypothesis. For the top ten and top fifty Web sites, concentration in political traffic is similar to traffic patterns for media sites and over the entire Web.[6]

Comparative Data, Comparative Metrics

Expectations that the Internet will produce a broad and flat distribution of audience attention are not borne out by these data. Yet the real test is comparative—data on Web audiences need to be placed alongside data from traditional media. In order to choose the most apt comparisons for online content, we need first to understand the ways in which the Internet has—and has not—changed the U.S. media environment.

Discussion of Internet politics has often left the impression that the Web has spurred a big shift in where the public gets its political information. In reality, surveys of media consumption show much less dramatic changes. One source of reliable data on citizens' changing media habits is the Pew Center for People and the Press (see discussion in Althaus 2007). Since 1991, national Pew surveys have asked Americans to list their two most important sources of news.[7] Especially crucial for our purposes, the Pew data predate

---

[6] Note that looking at the the top five hundred political sites is less meaningful for political Web sites, as this group includes more than half the tracked outlets.

[7] The exact wording of the Pew question is, "How have you been getting most of your news about national and international issues? From television, from newspapers, from radio, from magazines, or from the Internet?" Respondents are prompted, but not required, to list a second news source.

the emergence of the Internet as a mass medium. When the Pew survey first asked about Internet news sources in 1994, less than 1 percent of those surveyed listed the Internet as one of their primary news sources.

The Pew survey data do show some sudden shifts in the public's media diet in response to high-profile news events. Reliance on television jumped (and use of radio and newspapers fell) after the September 11 attacks, the invasion of Iraq, and Hurricane Katrina (Althaus 2007). Yet at no point over the past decade and a half has television's dominant position been challenged. By the end of 2006, three out of four respondents listed television as a main source of news—a rate basically unchanged from 1991 levels. While reliance on newspapers is substantially below the peak levels reported in the mid-1990s, the 2006 numbers show that two in five Americans still rely on newspapers as a major news source—only slightly below numbers from the pre-Internet era. By comparison, one in four of those surveyed by the end of 2006 listed the Internet as a major news source, and one in five relied on radio. While the Pew data show that the Internet has edged out radio in popularity since 2003, they also suggest that the audience for online news has been stable (or even declined slightly) in recent years (Pew Center for People and the Press 2006). As with newspapers, reliance on radio is not much below the levels of the early 1990s.

It is clear that so far, the Internet has had only modest success in displacing traditional media sources. Still, in order to compare online with off-line media, it makes sense to focus on print and radio, where the strongest case can be made that the Internet has stolen some audience (or at least some revenue) from traditional outlets.

There is, fortunately, a single authoritative source of data on print audiences. The Audit Bureau of Circulations (ABC) certifies circulation figures for nearly all major U.S. newspapers and magazines. The ABC data used here come from December 2003, and include 1,058 daily newspapers and 653 national magazines.[8] The radio data come from the Arbitron corporation, a major industry source for U.S. radio audience and demographic information. The Arbitron data include 1,290 radio stations in the

---

[8] Though more recent data are available for the top two hundred outlets (and are used below), these slightly older data include all magazines and newspapers tracked by ABC, not just the top one hundred or top two hundred outlets. For daily newspapers, the data reflect whichever day of the week has the highest circulation.

Table 5.2
Comparison of Audience Share, Print versus Digital

	Top 10	11–20	21–50	51–100	101–500	501+
News and media Web sites	29%	12%	10%	9%	23%	21%
vs. newspaper circulation	+10%	+2%	−7%	−6%	−7%	+12%
vs. magazine circulation	+2%	+3%	−6%	−6%	−8%	+20%

This table compares the distribution of audience share for news and media Web sites against circulation numbers for newspapers and magazines.

nation's top fifty radio markets. These fifty markets include more than 120 million Americans age twelve or older, roughly half the nation's twelve-and-older population.

All of these data are national, not regional, in scope. Radio stations in Cleveland and Baltimore cannot compete with each other for listeners, but every Web site in a given niche competes directly against all the rest. One aim of this analysis is to compare locally fragmented media against online content that does not face the same geographic restrictions.

When these print and radio data are placed alongside data from the Web, overall concentration looks surprisingly similar. Returning to table 5.1, the top ten newspapers receive 19 percent of the nation's newspaper circulation, and the top ten magazines receive 27 percent of magazine circulation. By comparison, the top ten Web sites receive 26 percent of all Web traffic; within news and media sites, 29 percent of traffic goes to the top ten outlets.

Perhaps the most interesting comparison is between newspaper circulation and traffic to news and media Web sites. In both cases, the top fifty outlets account for slightly less than half of the total market; yet the distribution of audience is different between the two media. Popular sites are more important online, but so are tiny sites. The most substantial difference comes from what might be termed "middle-class" outlets. Outlets ranked from 101 to 500 account for 35 percent of print newspaper readership, but only 22 percent of readership for media sites. And while papers below the top 500 represent only 9 percent of the nation's print circulation, 21 percent of media site visits go to outlets ranked 500 or below.

Table 5.2 offers another representation of these data. It again compares media Web site traffic to newspaper and magazine circulation, grouping outlets in categories ranked by popularity: the top 10 outlets, outlets 11 to 20, outlets 21 to 50, and so on. Row one presents the market share of these ranked categories for media sites. Rows two and three subtract the newspaper and magazine market share in these categories from the media Web site numbers.

Audience share among media sites is not more equal online—table 5.2 shows that the top 20 outlets grab more of the online market than they do in print media. But there are substantial drops in audience share for those media organizations in the middle categories—outlets ranked 21 to 500. Though the top media outlets online seem at least as important as those in print, audience share for small and middling outlets has been shifted downward. The smallest outlets have not taken over the media environment online. Instead, they seem to have cannibalized the audience of their moderately sized peers.

Metrics for Concentration

Looking at the market share of the top outlets is not the only way to measure concentration, and social scientists have long relied on more systematic measures to judge the gap between the resource rich and the resource poor. For our purposes, I adapt two of the most broadly used metrics in order to compare concentration across online and off-line media. I also apply a recently proposed metric developed specifically to measure media diversity.

The first of these metrics is the Gini coeffient. Originally developed in the early twentieth century to measure income inequality, Corrado Gini (1921) himself declared that the Gini coefficient could be used to calculate relative inequality for almost any resource. The Gini coefficient is equal to twice the area between the Lorenz curve and the (hypothetical) line of perfect equality.[9] There are many ways to calculate the Gini coefficient, but one of the most common formulas is provided by Malcolm Brown (1994). If X is the cumulative proportion of the population, and if Y is the

---

[9] The Lorenz curve can be obtained by plotting the cumulative distribution function of the resource in question against the cumulative distribution of the population possessing the resource. In a population governed by perfect equality, the Lorenz curve is a perfectly straight line: 30 percent of the population owns 30 percent of the wealth, 75 percent of the population owns 75 percent of the wealth, and so forth.

cumulative proportion of the resource in question, the Gini coefficient is equal to the following:

$$G = 1 - \sum_{i=0}^{k-1} (Y_{i+1} + Y_i)(X_{i+1} - X_i)$$

The Gini coefficient produces possible values between 0 and 1. Higher values correspond to greater inequality.

The second measure of inequality is the Herfindahl-Hirschman Index, or the HHI (Hirschman 1964). Developed to measure firm power within industries, the HHI is calculated by taking an observation's total resource share expressed as a percentage, squaring it, and taking the sum across all observations. More formally, the HHI can be calculated as:

$$HHI = \sum_{1}^{N} P_i^2,$$

where N is the number of outlets, and P_i is the percentage of total resources controlled by the ith media outlet or Web site. The HHI has possible values between 0 and 10,000.

Lastly, I use the Noam index, a recent metric proposed by Eli Noam that attempts to balance the market power of the largest players with the number of media outlets that reach a nontrivial audience. As Noam (2004) puts it, "One should not have to choose between a measure of market power (the HHI) or of pluralism (the number of voices) but ought to incorporate both." Noam's solution to this problem is to take the HHI and divide it by the square root of the number of media "voices" that reach 1 percent audience share in a given market. The Noam index is thus derived from the following equation:

$$Noam = \sum_{1}^{N} \frac{P_i^2}{\sqrt{\hat{N}}},$$

where P_i is the percentage of the total audience attracted by the ith media outlet, N is the number of outlets, and $\hat{N}$ is the number of outlets with at least a 1 percent market share. As Noam (2004) explains, "One per cent seems a reasonable floor: small but not trivial." As with the HHI, the Noam Index gives possible values between 0 and 10,000; however, all nonmonopoly markets will score lower on the Noam index than they do on the HHI.

The HHI and the Gini coefficient are the most commonly used metrics of inequality or concentration in the social sciences; the Noam index is too new to have seen much use. This set of measures is attractive in part because each differs in its emphases. The HHI, by squaring its components, focuses on the observations with the highest values. Smaller players receive almost no weight in calculating the HHI. The Gini coefficient, by contrast, is just a mean, and it is drawn equally from all observations in the data. Adding a large number of observations with small values raises the Gini coefficient dramatically.

The results of this analysis can be seen in table 5.3. Each of these metrics reinforces the conclusion that online audiences are at least as concentrated as those in traditional media.[10] The first column of the table shows the Gini coefficient across all of these media categories. For overall Web traffic, news and media sites, and sites focusing on politics, the Gini coefficient suggests greater inequality online than in print or radio.[11] Perhaps, one might suggest, an avalanche of small online publishers is pulling the average down, making it difficult to see that Internet audiences are spreading their attention across a broader set of outlets.

The second and third columns of table 5.3 show that this is not the case. Thousands of information producers with minuscule market share might alter the Gini coefficient, but would have no effect on the HHI. The HHI numbers indicate that traffic over the entire Web is about as concentrated as newspaper circulation. Within news and media Web sites, and within sites focusing on politics, the HHI actually exceeds that for magazines and newspapers. According to this metric, news and media consumption is more concentrated online than off-line.

The Noam index also finds comparable concentration between Web content and traditional media. The number of "voices" used in the Index—

---

[10] Two recent cross-media studies adopt similar metrics and reach similar conclusions. Jungsu Yim (2003) finds that in traditional media, concentration increases with the number of outlets available. Comparing the circulation figures of the top one hundred newspapers with the number of links their Web sites receive, James Hamilton (2004, chap. 7) suggests that the economics of producing online news may result in concentration rather than dispersion.

[11] One limitation of the Hitwise data is that traffic numbers are only given for sites that have more than 0.01 percent of the category's total visits. The Gini coefficient can only be calculated using sites above this threshold, reducing the N in the "All Web sites" category to 1,346, in the "News and media" category to 1,810, and in the "Politics" category to 558. This constraint does make the Gini coefficient numbers more comparable across media, however. This lower N also likely reduces the level of inequality reported, making our comparison here a conservative one.

Table 5.3
Three Metrics of Media Concentration

	Gini coeff.	HHI	Noam index
All Web sites	.76	69	22
News and media sites	.88	134	40
Political sites	.85	140	31
Radio audience	.53	19	—
Newspaper circulation	.69	73	18
Magazine circulation	.70	123	34

This table summarizes three metrics of media concentration across both online and traditional content. Overall, it finds that online audiences are at least as concentrated as audiences for off-line media. No single radio station reached the Noam index's 1 percent threshold, and so the Noam index could not be calculated for radio audiences.

outlets reaching 1 percent market share—seems little different on the Web than in print. Nine Web sites have at least 1 percent of all Internet traffic, along with eleven news and media sites, and twenty-one political sites; this compares to sixteen newspapers and thirteen magazines that have at least 1 percent of national circulation. The number of outlets online is far greater than in traditional media, but the number reaching a "not trivial" audience has not budged.

Newspaper Concentration in Print and Pixels

These data and metrics point to consistent conclusions. Yet a radio station is not interchangeable with a newsmagazine, and neither is exactly equivalent to a Web site. Ideally, we would like to isolate the effects of the distribution medium from other factors—to examine the same content, produced by the same organizations, distributed both online and off-line.

One segment of the media lends itself to such a comparison: newspapers. Of the nation's two hundred most widely circulated newspapers, all now publish their content on the World Wide Web, either on their own Web sites or on a site shared with another news organization. With only a handful of exceptions, newspaper Web sites overwhelmingly present the same articles, prepared by the same staff, as the paper's print edition. To be sure, many newpapers have *tried* to extend themselves beyond just posting online versions of their print editions; yet as Pablo Boczkowski (2005) shows, few of these efforts have met with success. Scholars have long portrayed newspapers as big organizations with entrenched bureaucracies (see, for example, Epstein 1974), and this fact has been painfully evident in newspaper responses to the Internet phenomenon.

To make this comparison, I gathered February 2006 data from the ABC, looking at the top two hundred daily newspapers by circulation. I then gathered Hitwise visitor data from the same month for these newspapers' Web sites, and applied the same metrics used above.[12] The results can be seen in table 5.4. Across every measure, newspaper content is more concentrated online than in print. The top ten outlets control more of the total market, and the Gini coefficient for Web site traffic is larger than that for circulation. The HHI and Noam index are twice as large for the online data.

A closer look shows that online distribution has benefited some types of newspapers far more than others. According to Hitwise, the *New York Times* and the *Washington Post* have online traffic roughly 2.5 times their share of the print newspaper market. The *Boston Globe* and the *San Francisco Chronicle* double their online market share in comparison to their print circulation. One newspaper—the *Washington Times*—does even better. A conservative paper based in the nation's capital, the *Washington Times* has a weekday circulation of less than a hundred thousand. The paper's extensive coverage of national politics from a right-leaning perspective, however, has earned it an online readership three times larger than its share of the print market.[13]

Yet among the rest of the outlets, the story is far different. More than two-thirds of newspapers attract a smaller share of online traffic than print circulation. It is disproportionately local, smaller-circulation papers that are weaker online. Papers like the *Wilmington Star-News* and the *Provo Daily Herald* face much tougher challenges on the Web than does the *New York Times* or the *Washington Post*.

Overall, these data suggest that there is a trade-off between competing democratic values. We want citizens to have access to the nation's best newspapers, no matter where they live. At the same time, geographic

[12] Fifteen smaller newspapers are omitted from the data below, because their official Web sites are produced in partnership with larger newspapers. Additional analyses were performed with just the top one hundred newspapers (which did not include any missing data), and with the missing newspapers replaced by the next fifteen lower-ranking sites. In both cases, the substantive results were identical to those presented in table 5.4. Note that the Gini coefficient is the only metric likely to be affected by such missing data.

[13] The *Washington Times* is the only such outlier in the sample.

Table 5.4
Metrics of Concentration for Newspapers

	Top 10	Gini	HHI	Noam
Newspapers—Print circulation (top 200)	30%	.50	143	33
Newspapers—Web site visits (top 200)	42%	.62	304	65

This table summarizes metrics of concentration for newspapers, both online and in print. Even when comparing the same news organizations across the two media, online content shows substantially higher levels of concentration by every measure.

barriers that used to limit most communities to a handful of broadcast stations and a single local paper did serve to protect media diversity at the national level.

A Narrower Net

Many recent conversations about the Internet and media concentration have been framed by talk of the "long tail." Popularized by technology journalist Chris Anderson, the notion behind the long tail is that media is moving from a model of scarcity to a model of plenty. Traditional retailers (such as Blockbuster Video) have limited shelf space, so they can only afford to carry the most popular titles; yet online companies (such as Netflix) can offer far broader selections. Instead of "squeezing millions from a few megahits at the top of the charts," the Internet allows producers to exploit "the millions of niche markets at the shallow end of the bitstream" (Anderson 2004). Anderson (2006a) claims that "all those niches can potentially add up to a market that is as big as (if not bigger than) the hits."

The long tail represents a rebranding and refinement of claims that the Internet promotes narrowcasting at the expense of mass media. For our purposes here, I will set aside talk about music, movies, or books; perhaps in these areas Anderson's arguments do hold (though some have been skeptical). Yet many, including Anderson himself, have applied the same principles to news audiences and political discourse (Reynolds and Reynolds 2006).[14]

---

[14] Top blogger Glenn Reynolds states that Anderson's book "has a pretty strong Army of Davids resonance in places" (Reynolds and Reynolds 2006); Anderson (2006b) similarly remarks on "how well my thesis and that of [Reynolds's book] *An Army of Davids* dovetail."

This chapter suggests that there are problems with this sort of thinking. First, there is the economics of content production. Some types of content are cheap to produce; some are not. Talk about the long tail or narrow-casting is irrelevant to online markets where the barriers to entry remain high. Almost by definition, mass media is expensive to produce but cheap to distribute, guaranteeing large economies of scale for the most successful outlets. If the Internet lowers distribution costs still further, the forces that created media concentration in print and on the airwaves still remain.

We have seen that political content is a niche market within the broader Web. News and media Web sites and political Web sites are the categories of content most relevant for politics, and for both groups it is hardly true that the tail of the distribution adds up to half of the total market. It is possible, as we saw in chapters 3 and 4, to break these broader political niches down into subcategories and sub-subcategories of content, looking just at liberal sites, just at sites on Congress or gun control, or just at pro- or antiabortion sites. Yet the ability to subdivide the Web into millions of niches does not guarantee an egalitarian outcome, any more than Zeno's paradox guarantees that an arrow in flight will never hit its target.

The biggest story here is not the long tail but what we might call the "missing middle." From the beginning, the Internet has been portrayed as a media Robin Hood—robbing audience from the big print and broadcast outlets, and giving it to the little guys. But the data in this chapter suggest that audiences are moving in both directions. On the one hand, the news market in cyberspace seems even more concentrated on the top ten or twenty outlets than print media is. On the other, the tiniest outlets have indeed earned a substantial portion of the total eyeballs. News and media sites ranked five hundred or below, for example, receive 23 percent of the category's traffic, far more than in any traditional media. It is the middle-class outlets that have seen relative decline in the online world. Moreover, it is overwhelmingly smaller, local media organizations that have lost out to national sources.

These findings contradict the more simplistic narratives that continue to dominate public discourse. For example, not long ago the editorial board of the *New York Times* argued that the Internet had made A. J. Liebling's famous aphorism about the freedom of the press obsolete:

> Freedom of the press, so the saying goes, belongs only to those
> who own one. Radio and television are controlled by those rich

enough to buy a broadcast license. But anyone with an Internet-connected computer can reach out to a potential audience of billions. (A. Cohen 2006)

Like much else written about the Internet, the *Times'* statement is both technically correct and misleading. The Internet does provide any citizen a *potential* audience of billions, in the same way that *potentially* anyone can win the lottery. In their enthusiasm, many have forgotten to do the math, and that math shows that the odds of hitting it big online are vanishingly small. Individually, each of the myriad sources that make up the long tail are insignificant; even together, they remain only a fraction of the content that citizens actually see.

In a world with thousands of news sources only a few clicks away, many assumed that organizations like CNN or the *New York Times* would become less important. For those concerned that the Internet will destroy general-interest intermediaries, the continuing strength of large, national, name-brand news outlets is welcome. Whether a sharper divide between big and small outlets is good news for other democratic values—media diversity, a broad public sphere, and equal participation in civic debates—is a more doubtful prospect.

Six

Blogs: The New Elite Media

The flaw in the pluralist heaven is that the heavenly chorus
sings with a strong upper-class accent.

—E. E. Schattschneider, *The Semi-Sovereign People*, 1960

Those who have been enthused about the Internet's political implications, as well as those who have looked at the new medium suspiciously, have begun by assuming that the Internet will funnel the attention of the public away from traditional news outlets and interest groups and toward countless small-scale sources of political information. As previous chapters have shown, this assumption is problematic. Winners-take-all patterns in the ecology of the Web—both in its link structure and traffic—do not fit with what many have assumed.

Nonetheless, the concentration we find online does not mean that the Internet merely supports politics as usual. I began by looking at the role of the Internet in Dean's presidential campaign. This chapter looks at the rise of blogs—another area of U.S. politics where the Internet has brought dramatic changes.

Weblogs or blogs—first-person, frequently updated online journals presented in reverse chronological order—are a new feature of the political landscape. Virtually unknown during the 2000 election cycle, by 2004 these online diaries garnered millions of readers and received extensive coverage in traditional media. Most have assumed that blogs are empowering ordinary citizens, and expanding the social and ideological diversity of the voices that find an audience. Stories of "ordinary" citizens catapulted to prominence by their blogging have been told and retold. Some have even suggested that blogging and "citizen journalism" will displace the "elite" or "old" media.

This chapter begins by examining recent data on the extent to which Americans read and create blogs, and goes on to explore claims that blogs are reshaping political communication. Both praise and condemnation of blogging depend on widely shared beliefs about who reads blogs, and who writes them.

Many of these beliefs are mistaken. In the last part of the chapter, I gather systematic data on those bloggers who reach a substantial audience. Bloggers fit poorly into the narrative that has been constructed for them. Though millions of Americans now maintain a blog, only a few dozen political bloggers get as many readers as a typical college newspaper. Yet the problem is not just the small number of voices that matter; it is that those voices are quite unrepresentative of the broader electorate.

Partly because of their intensely personal nature, blogs present an important case study in online speech, and in understanding whose voices matter online. Ultimately, blogs have given a small group of educational, professional, and technical elites new influence in U.S. politics. Blogs have done far less to amplify the political voice of average citizens.

Blogs Hit the Big Time

Of all the changes in the media environment between the 2000 and 2004 elections, the growth of blogs ranks among the biggest. At the end of 2000, few Americans had heard the term blog. By the end of the 2004 election cycle, discussions of political blogging were difficult to ignore.

If we want to understand blog influence on the 2004 campaign, one place to start is by examining nationwide surveys conducted after the election. Two national telephone surveys were conducted by the Pew Internet and American Life Project in November 2004 (Ranie 2005); an additional nationwide telephone survey was conducted in February 2005 by Gallup (Saad 2005). According to the Pew surveys, of the roughly 120 million Americans online, 7 percent—or 8 million people total—had themselves created a blog. Twenty-seven percent of Internet users reported reading blogs, making 32 million Americans blog readers. Gallup similarly found that 15 percent of the public read blogs at least a few times a month; 12 percent read political blogs this often.

Compared to traditional outlets such as newspapers and television news, blogs remained niche players. Two percent of the Gallup respondents visited political blogs daily, an additional 4 percent visited several times a week, and 6 percent more visited a few times a month; 77 percent never visited political blogs. The Pew results were similar: 4 percent of Internet users reported reading political blogs "regularly" during the campaign; an additional 5 percent reported that they "sometimes" read political blogs. Even among Internet users, 62 percent of the Pew respondents did not "have a good idea" of what a blog was. Fifty-six percent of the Gallup sample was "not at all familiar" with blogs.

Still, blogging has grown rapidly for a form of publishing that only began in 2000 and 2001. In June 2002, a Pew survey found that 3 percent of Internet users were bloggers. By early 2004, that number had jumped to 5 percent of Internet users, and to 7 percent by November 2004. The growth of blog readership was even more rapid. In spring 2003, 11 percent of Internet users reported reading blogs; by February 2004, that number was 17 percent. In November 2004, 27 percent of Internet users were blog readers—a growth of 56 percent in just nine months. Not all of this readership, of course, was focused on political blogs.

Both blog publishing and readership continued to grow rapidly after the 2004 election. A Pew telephone survey conducted in April 2006 found that 8 percent of Internet users—12 million U.S. adults—maintained a blog (Lenhart and Fox 2006). A stunning 39 percent of Internet users, or 57 million citizens, reported that they read blogs. Eleven percent of bloggers stated that politics was the main topic of their online journals; if accurate, this estimate would put the number of political blogs at about 1.3 million.

According to the Pew report, bloggers are evenly split betweeen men and women; roughly half are thirty years of age or younger. Bloggers are more highly educated than the public at large, with 37 percent of the sample having earned a bachelor's degree. Perhaps most important, 38 percent of bloggers are knowledge-based professional workers, compared with 16 percent in the population as a whole.

While the Pew and Gallup data illustrate the broad contours of blog readership, data from Hitwise allow us to examine the demographics of those who read the most popular political blogs. Table 6.1 shows that there is a gender divide between liberal and conservative blogs. While the top liberal blogs on this list have a male readership of between 32 and 55 percent, conservative blog readership varies from 53 to 89 percent male. Hitwise data show, too, the breakdown of blog readership by age. For each of these blogs, between two-thirds and four-fifths of their readership is

Table 6.1
Gender of Visitors to Political Blogs

Rank	Blog	Male readership (%)
1	*Daily Kos*	47%
2	Instapundit	59%
3	*Eschaton (Atrios)*	52%
4	Michelle Malkin	57%
5	*Crooks and Liars*	32%
6	Little Green Footballs	89%
7	PowerLine	74%
8	RedState.org	68%
9	*Wonkette*	46%
10	Andrew Sullivan	53%
11	*Kevin Drum*	55%
12	Hugh Hewitt	80%

This table presents Hitwise data on the gender of blog visitors for a set of top political Web blogs for October 2005. Liberal bloggers are in italics. Though we would expect that conservative blogs would have higher male readership, the extent of the disparity is surprising.

thirty-five or older. Table 6.2 lays out these results in detail. Chapter 4 suggested that visits to political Web sites were dominated by older Web users. While young people seem more likely to visit these blogs than they are to visit other sorts of political sites, the average blog here gets half of its readership from those forty-five or older.

The overall picture, therefore, shows blogs to be a small but rapidly growing part of the media environment. There are important differences between the profile of those who create blogs and that of the general public. But as we shall see, the differences between bloggers and the wider public pales in comparison to the gap between the few dozen political bloggers who find a large audience, and the hundreds of thousands of bloggers who do not.

Bloggers and the Media

Blogs are so new that little has been published by academics about their political implications. Scholars who have examined blogging have focused on a number of consistent themes. Some have looked at two basic questions: Do blogs matter, and if so, how? The answer offered seems to be "yes," that

Table 6.2
Age of Visitors to Political Blogs

Rank	Blog	18–34	35–44	45–54	55+
1	Daily Kos	34%	13%	29%	24%
2	Instapundit	29%	22%	20%	29%
3	Eschaton (Atrios)	26%	29%	31%	14%
4	Michelle Malkin	19%	29%	19%	33%
5	Crooks and Liars	29%	16%	30%	26%
6	Little Green Footballs	26%	22%	20%	32%
7	PowerLine	21%	16%	24%	40%
8	RedState.org	29%	26%	26%	20%
9	Wonkette	28%	19%	41%	12%
10	Andrew Sullivan	31%	34%	12%	13%
11	Kevin Drum	22%	24%	23%	30%
12	Hugh Hewitt	31%	23%	25%	21%
	Average	27%	23%	25%	25%

The table presents Hitwise data on the age of visitors to prominent political blogs, as of October 2005. Because of rounding, each row may not add up to exactly 100 percent. The central finding here is that blog readership is not just limited to the young. On average, half of the readership to these blogs comes from those forty-five and older.

top blogs reach a small but influential audience, and that powerful insights trickle up to these top outlets (Drezner and Farrell 2004a; Bloom and Kernel 2003; Benkler 2006). Others have examined blogging's ability to democratize political content creation (Chadwick 2006), and the implications of this for truth claims and perceptions of credibility (Johnson and Kaye 2004; Matheson 2004). Research by Lada Adamic and Natalie Glance (2005) has also looked at patterns of linkage among political blogs; among other things, Adamic and Glance found levels of liberal-conservative cross-linkage far higher than that found in the traffic patterns detailed above.

The relatively small volume of academic writing has been counterbalanced by an avalanche of debate in the popular press. This surge of interest in blogs can be charted by the number of stories about them in major newspapers (table 6.3). The earliest mention of blogs in the Lexis-Nexis database is not until 1999. In the whole of 2000, there were only nine references to blogs in their current meaning as online journals. In 2001, blogging tools became more widely available to the public through the efforts of companies like Blogger.com; much of the early coverage of blogs

Table 6.3
Number of Newspaper Stories about Blogs

Year	No. of newspaper stories
1999	3
2000	9
2001	209
2002	408
2003	1442
2004	3212

This table presents the number of stories in major papers that contain references to "Weblog" or "blog." (Several references to blog as a British slang word have been omitted in the 1999 and 2000 data.) *Source*: Lexis-Nexis.

focused on their social implications. The real explosion in news coverage of blogs, though, was spurred by politics. In 2003, as Dean's insurgent campaign for president took off, blogs were given much of the credit.

If we are to understand the relationship between blogs and politics, it is worth cataloging the expectations about blogging in media reports. Partly, this is to get a broader view of claims about blogging than is provided by the few academic articles on the subject. Yet another rationale is even more basic. Blogs are important, scholars have argued, because public discourse matters. If this is true, then it is worth cataloging the themes that have dominated public debates about blogging.

This section thus examines the claims made about political blogging in newspapers and periodicals. Thanks to electronic indexes, much of this writing is easily searchable. This chapter sifts through *all* the Lexis-Nexis articles between 1999 (when the word blog was coined) and the end of 2004 that mention any variant of the words blog and politics. In total, I examined more than 300 news articles in major papers, and more than 150 articles in magazines and journals. Discussions about blogs in print have been remarkably consistent, returning again and again to the same themes and concerns.

"Ordinary Citizens"

The central claim about blogs in public discourse is that they amplify the political voice of ordinary citizens. Almost everything written about blogs has explored this belief. Most often, the mood is upbeat: "You, too, can have a voice in Blogland" (Campbell 2002); "[blogs] enable anyone with an opinion to be heard" (Megna 2002). As the *Washington Post* explained, "When you have a theory or a concern [you can] put it on your blog and you can tell the whole world" (McCarthy 2004). This vision of blogs is often fit into a larger framework of Internet empowerment: "[Blogs] allow anyone with an opinion the ability [to] reach millions of people instantly and simultaneously" (Bartlett 2003).

These claims about blogging are so standard that they have given birth to their own genre, what might be termed the Joe Average Blogger feature. Such articles begin by producing a citizen of the most ordinary sort. Personal characteristics that argue against political influence, such as youth or a blue-collar profession, are emphasized. The moral is political empowerment: one citizen who suddenly has a voice in the political arena thanks to his or her blog. Numerous examples of this genre can be found (see, for example, Weiss 2003; Falcone 2003; Kessler 2004; McCarthy 2004).

Such optimistic narratives have not gone entirely unchallenged. Coverage has noted that "some skeptics question whether every supporter's passing thought deserves a public platform" (Weiss 2003). Others have made fun of bloggers when they write—literally—about what they had for lunch (Hartlaub 2004a). As one reporter put it, "Ordinary people writing unpaid about things that matter to them may mark a crucial change in the information landscape; it can also be skull-crushingly dull" (MacIntyre 2004).

Still, few have disputed the notion that blogs are making political discourse less exclusive. As an executive producer at MSNBC explained, "It lets some other voices and ideas into that airless room that the media has become" (Campbell 2002). Blogs have been hailed as "harbingers of a new, interactive culture that will change the way democracy works, turning voters into active participants rather than passive consumers, limiting the traditional media's role as gatekeeper, and giving the rank-and-file voter unparalleled influence" (Weiss 2003). As one blogger observed in the *Los Angeles Times*, "Bloggers are about providing more points of view, about providing those points of view in an authentic and personal voice" (Stone 2004).

Diversity in the blogosphere is thus taken for granted. This new form of political expression is "fabulously unscripted," and "spans a spectrum of beliefs and interests as diverse as the Web itself " (Stone 2004). Because bloggers are nothing more than average citizens, "the universe of permissible opinions will expand, unconstrained by the prejudices, tastes or interests of the old media elite" (Last 2002).

Do Blogs Matter? Lott, Dean, and Rather

Judging from popular press coverage, then, blogging is the second coming of online politics—the Internet redistributing political power to the grass roots (or as many bloggers call themselves, the "netroots"). This claim was reiterated at moments when bloggers' writings seemed to impact broader political concerns. Arguably the first instance of this grew from an unlikely source: a birthday party. Senate Majority Leader Trent Lott, in remarks at Senator Strom Thurmond's hundredth birthday celebration, noted that Lott's home state of Mississippi was "proud" to have voted for Thurmond during his 1948 run for president on a segregationist platform. Lott stated that if Thurmond had won, "We wouldn't have had all of these problems over the years." Though Lott's remarks were delivered live on C-SPAN, most news organizations ignored them. Blogs were given the credit for refusing to let the issue die (see, for example, von Sternberg 2004). Conservative bloggers such as Andrew Sullivan and Instapundit's Glenn Reynolds condemned Lott's comments; liberal bloggers such as Joshua Micah Marshall and Atrios highlighted previous remarks by Lott that seemed to approve of segregation. When Lott issued a weak apology early the following week, a cascade of coverage followed, ultimately forcing Lott to resign his leadership position. Assessments of blogs' part in Lott's resignation remain controversial.[1]

---

[1] One popular account concluded afterward that "never before have [blogs] owned a story like they did the Trent Lott saga" (Fasoldt 2003); top blogger Markos Moulitsas Zuniga likewise declared, "The point when I knew we had an impact is when we got Trent Lott fired" (Nevius 2004; see also Smolkin 2004; Kornblum 2003). Political scientist Joel Bloom (2003) argues that it was bloggers' persistent coverage of the issue that transformed it from an ignored story to a front-page issue. Daniel Drezner and Henry Farrell (2004a) also assign blogs a critical role in the Lott affair, asserting that journalistic readership made blogs an important driver of mainstream media coverage (see also Ashbee 2003). Yet other scholars have been more cautious. Noting that the *Washington Post* and ABC News did cover the story within thirty-six hours of the event, Esther Scott concludes that "how much of the story made its way from the blogs—as opposed to other Internet sources, such as [ABC News'] *The Note*—into the mainstream is difficult to determine" (2004, 23). Blogger Kevin Drum, himself credited with a significant role in the Lott affair, ultimately argues for a similar conclusion. Says Drum (2005), "I suspect that blogs played a role in the Trent Lott affair, but not as big a role as we think."

Political blogs were also credited with a key role in online campaigning during the 2004 electoral cycle. Numerous articles highlighted the importance of blogs in Dean's online efforts (see, for example, Baker, Green, and Hof 2004). Bloggers were seen as a new source of money for congressional candidates (Faler 2004b; Lillkvist 2004; Martinez 2004). The Democratic Party's decision to give thirty-six bloggers media credentials at the 2004 Democratic National Convention was declared a "watershed" (Perrone 2004), and was widely covered.[2]

But the single most important incident in winning the blogosphere respect was the scandal that some bloggers branded as "Rathergate." On September 8, 2004, CBS News broadcast a report on George W. Bush's Vietnam era Air National Guard service. CBS claimed to have unearthed documents showing that Bush had failed to fulfill his military obligations. Late that night, an anonymous member of FreeRepublic.com, a right-wing forum, wrote that the CBS documents couldn't have come from an early 1970s typewriter. Early the next morning, Power Line, the second-most-trafficked conservative blog, linked to this posting; Charles Johnson, proprietor of the third-largest conservative blog, soon posted documents typed in Microsoft Word that he alleged matched the disputed documents. Much traditional media coverage followed, and CBS ultimately conceded that it could not verify the documents' authenticity. Dan Rather announced his resignation as the CBS news anchor a few months later.

In the media postmortems that followed, bloggers were given the starring role. The headline in the *New York Times* declared, "No Disputing It: Blogs Are Major Players" (Wallsten 2004b). According to many, Rather's troubles put mainstream media on notice: the distributed network of bloggers functioned as a "truth squad" adept at "double-checking and counterpunching the mainstream media" (Web of Politics 2004; Seper 2004b). As political scientist Daniel Drezner explained, "A couple of the blogs raised factual questions—it was like firing a flare. Then the mainstream journalists did the heavy lifting. It was highly symbiotic" (quoted in von Sternberg 2004). Even the lowliest online activist might trigger a cybercascade powerful enough to bring down a national political leader. As one Democratic activist declared, "It was amazing Thursday to watch the documents story go from [a comment on] FreeRepublic.com, a bastion

---

[2] See, for example, Hartlaub 2004a; Perrone 2004; Halloran 2004; Memmott 2004.

of right-wing lunacy, to Drudge to the mainstream media in less than 12 hours" (Wallsten 2004b).

Taken together, the Dean campaign and the Lott and Rather resignations convinced many skeptics that blogs were worth paying attention to. As one pundit remarked, "I've had my doubts about Web logs . . . [but] I've changed my mind, big time" (Taube 2004). Blogs, the argument went, had come to set the agenda for other media "in a way not unlike talk radio" (Fasoldt 2003). Blogs allowed "issues and ideas . . . [to] remain in the public's mind for months longer" (Seper 2004a). And although most of the general public didn't read blogs, those who did ranked among the most influential citizens. As the *Washington Post* summarized, blog readers "tend to be white, well-educated and, disproportionately, opinion leaders in their social circles" (Faler 2004a). A wide assortment of political elites themselves—from opinion journalists like Paul Krugman to political operatives like former Clinton adviser Simon Rosenberg and Dean campaign manager Joe Trippi—proclaimed themselves addicted to blogs (Scott 2004; Morse 2004; Trippi 2005).

Partisanship and Inaccuracy

By the end of the 2004 election cycle, then, most public discussion took it for granted that blogs had become a crucial part of the political landscape. There was also much agreement on how blogs wielded political influence: by setting the broader media agenda, and reaching an elite audience of opinion leaders and (especially) journalists. Yet grudging respect for blogs coexisted uneasily with concern about what blogging meant for political discourse. Again and again, journalists claimed that blogs had two central failings. First, they suggested that blogs were sensational and inaccurate. Second, they argued that the partisan nature of blogs poisoned public debate. These criticisms, in large part, depended on assumptions about bloggers' backgrounds.

Much vitriol was directed at bloggers for their salaciousness and ostensible inaccuracy. As bloggers became accredited journalists at the Democratic National Convention, one newspaper editorialized that "they would be wise to start putting a higher premium on accuracy" (Blog-Hopping 2004). One reporter declared that bloggers were "like C-SPAN in the hands of a 19-year-old" (Wood 2004). The *American Prospect*'s Natasha Berger railed against "the serious problem of quality control in the increasingly powerful blogging world" (quoted in Seipp 2002). For some, blogs inspired even harsher language. "Political blogs have crawled from the Web's primordial ooze ... bloggers—often partisans—can spin the news till they get vertigo, free from the clutches of (a) an editor and (b) the truth" (Manuel 2004). In one oft-referenced remark, Jonathan Klein (subsequently the president of CNN) declared that "you couldn't have a starker contrast between the multiple layers of checks and balances [of network news organizations] and a guy sitting in his living room in his pajamas writing" (Colford 2004).

Bloggers may have caught flaws in CBS's coverage, but journalists were quick to pounce when bloggers fell short of journalistic standards. When the Drudge Report claimed that John Kerry had had an extramarital affair, the allegations quickly migrated to Wonkette.com and other blogs (Smolkin 2004).[3] Blogs also incubated rumors about Kerry's military record that were picked up—and largely discredited—by the mainstream press (von Sternberg 2004).[4] Similarly, on election day 2004, several top bloggers posted early—and misleading—exit poll results that seemed to show Kerry headed for victory (Horn 2004; Hartlaub 2004b). After the exit poll incident, blogger Ana Marie Cox commented, "All of a sudden blogs were back to being the pajama-clad amateurs" (quoted in Bishop 2004).

Closely tied to concerns about blogs' accuracy are worries about their partisanship. As one *New York Times* article defined it, this is "the very nature of the blog—all spin, all the time" (Williams 2004). Many argued that "it is a dangerous mistake to grant the usually partisan bloggers the privileges of more mainstream journalists" (Yeager 2004). *Washington Post* columnist Robert J. Samuelson (2004) derided blogs as "the fast food of the news business," and contended that blogs made news "more selective and slanted." One editorial board similarly worried that "depending on your reading habits, you may not get to the truth, but only a series of opinions that fit your point of view" (Seper 2004a).

---

[3] Mainstream news organizations largely dropped the issue after both Kerry and the woman named denied any relationship.

[4] In a matter with fewer electoral consequences, a link from Wonkette also helped to expose the story of Jessica Cutler, a congressional staffer who wrote an anonymous blog detailing her sexual escapades on the Hill, including what she alleged were dalliances with a married Bush administration official (Rosen 2004). In the miniscandal that followed, Cutler's identity was exposed, she was fired from her job, given a book contract, and ultimately ended up posing nude for *Playboy* magazine.

So You Want to Be a Blogger

Popular blog coverage has thus presented a consistent narrative of how and why blogs matter in U.S. politics. At the heart of these descriptions is the notion that blogging is making political discourse less exclusive, giving ordinary citizens an expanded political voice. Criticisms of blogging have been a mirror image of this same claim. Blogging, in the view of critics, is *too* democratic: it empowers the unqualified and the insipid, tramples on norms of accuracy and objectivity, and replaces trained professionals with partisan hacks.

In a technical sense, it is true that blogging allows a large group of citizens to air their opinions in public. But the more important question is not who posts on blogs but who actually gets read. The remainder of this chapter is focused on this question: Who *does* get heard in the blogosphere? First, how many political bloggers have managed to assemble more than a modest audience? Second, what are the characteristics of this group of successful bloggers?

Room at the Top?

Chapters 3 and 5 suggested that online political communities have highly skewed distributions of links and traffic, and the same pattern holds with political blogs. N. Z. Bear's Blogosphere Ecosystem project tracks five thousand of the most widely read blogs, compiling data from the SiteMeter tracking service used by many (though not all) bloggers (Bear 2004). The most popular blogs in this listing receive several hundred thousand visits daily, while the least popular receive ten daily visitors. In early March 2005, the most popular blog—Markos Moulitsas Zuniga's DailyKos .com—by itself accounted for 10 percent of all blog traffic in the sample. The top five blogs, taken together, account for 28 percent of blog traffic; the top ten blogs accounted for 48 percent. All sites with more than two thousand visits a day—the standard used for the broader survey below—got 74 percent of the traffic within the sample.

It has often been observed that voice in the blogosphere is highly personal. One place to begin, then, is to take a look at the most popular A-list bloggers. The following are brief profiles of the top ten political bloggers by audience, according to Bear's traffic numbers, as of early December 2004. Bloggers who do not use SiteMeter to track visitors to their site are not included in these rankings. Though the rankings for the top ten have been reasonably stable, this list should be taken as a snapshot, not as an authoritative catalog.

1. Markos Moulitsas Zuniga, a thirty-two-year-old lawyer and democratic political consultant, is proprietor of Daily Kos, the most trafficked political blog in the world. He graduated with a journalism degree from Northern Illinois University, where he edited the student newspaper, and earned a law degree at Boston University. Half Greek and half Salvadoran, Moulitsas spent part of his childhood in El Salvador, and served a three-year enlistment in the U.S. Army. Moulitsas lives in Berkeley, California.

2. University of Tennessee law professor Glenn Reynolds, forty-four, is the author of the conservative site Instapundit. Reynolds grew up as "a grad-student and faculty brat," and lived in Dallas, Cambridge, and Heidelberg before returning to Tennessee (Geras 2004). He holds a BA from the University of Tennessee, and a JD from Yale. Reynolds lives in Knoxville, Tennessee.

3. The blog Eschaton is published by Atrios—the pseudonym of Duncan Black, thirty-two, a former economics professor. Black earned a PhD in economics from Brown University, and has held research or teaching positions at the London School of Economics, the University of California at Irvine, and Bryn Mawr College. Before blogging, Black had extensive experience in grassroots activism. Black is currently a senior fellow at Media Matters for America, a left-leaning media watchdog organization. He lives in center city Philadelphia.

4. Charles Johnson, fifty-one, is a Web designer and former professional jazz guitarist who created the conservative blog Little Green Footballs (LGF). After his jazz career (which included several appearances on recordings that went gold), Johnson started CodeHead Software. He and his brother later started a Web design firm; the original LGF blog started as a test bed for the company's design work. Johnson lives in Los Angeles.

5. Thirty-five-year-old Joshua Micah Marshall, a professional journalist, publishes the liberal blog TalkingPointsMemo.com. Marshall earned a bachelor's degree from Princeton University and a PhD in early American history from Brown University. He served as editor at the *American Prospect*, and has written for beltway-focused publications

such the *Washington Monthly* and *The Hill*. At the time that this survey was conducted, Marshall lived in Washington, DC; he has since moved to New York City.

6. As of December 2004, the only woman blogger on SiteMeter's top ten list was Ana Marie Cox, thirty-one. Cox attended the University of Chicago and the University of Texas at Austin, and did graduate work at the University of California at Berkeley. During the Internet boom, Cox was the executive editor of the influential Internet journal Suck.com; she then worked as a writer and editor at the *American Prospect*, *Mother Jones*, and the *Chronicle of Higher Education*. The Wonkette blog is actually owned by Nick Denton, one of the creators of BlogAds, a blog advertising service. Cox lives in a suburb of Washington, DC.

7. PowerLine, a right-wing blog, is run by three undergraduate Dartmouth alumni: John Hinderaker, Scott Johnson, and Paul Mirengoff. All three are lawyers: Hinderaker has his JD from Harvard Law School, Johnson from the University of Minnesota, and Mirengoff from Stanford University. Before blogging, Hinderaker and Johnson had written political commentary together for more than a decade. Hinderaker and Johnson live in the Minneapolis–Saint Paul area; Mirengoff lives in Washington, DC.

8. Forty-six-year-old Kevin Drum, a former software consultant and technology executive, is another prominent blogger. Drum's father was a professor of Speech Communications at California State University at Long Beach; his mother taught elementary "gifted and talented" programs. Drum started college at Caltech as a math major, but transferred to California State University at Long Beach, where he edited the college newspaper and graduated with a degree in journalism. His most recent corporate position was as the vice president of marketing at a software firm, followed by several years of software consulting. Drum started the blog Calpundit in August 2002; in early 2004, the *Washington Monthly* hired Drum to move his blog onto its newly renovated Web site. He lives in Orange County, California.

9. Andrew Sullivan, forty-two, is the former editor in chief of the *New Republic*. Sullivan has written for numerous publications, including the *Sunday Times* (London), and the *New York Times*. Born in southern England, Sullivan did his undergraduate work at Oxford

University, where he was president of the prestigious Oxford Union debating society. He holds both an MPA and a PhD in government from Harvard University. Sullivan lives in Washington, DC.

10. Hugh Hewitt, a professor of law at Chapman University and a nationally syndicated radio host, runs the blog HughHewitt.com. Hewitt won three Emmys during ten years as the cohost of *Life and Times*, a nightly news and public affairs program sponsored by Los Angeles' PBS affiliate KCET. He has published several books. Hewitt graduated from Harvard College and earned his JD from Harvard Law School.

If we want to know how blogging has altered political voice, one place to start is by asking where these now-very-public individuals would be without their blogs. The short time frame makes counterfactuals easier. In a world without blogs, Drum would likely still be working as a software consultant; Johnson would be just another Los Angeles–based Web designer. Blogging has given a prominent platform to several individuals whose political writing might otherwise have been limited to a few letters to the editor. Yet from a broader perspective, blogging appears far less accessible. Sullivan and Hewitt were public figures long before they began blogging.

These top ten bloggers force us to reconsider claims that bloggers lack the training and norms of traditional journalists. In fact, five of these ten individuals—Marshall, Cox, Drum, Sullivan, and Hewitt—are current or former professional journalists from traditional news organizations.[5] For those who have continued to work as journalists, there is some evidence that their employers hold them accountable for what they write on their personal Web sites. For example, Sullivan reported that he had been "banished" from his job writing for the *New York Times Magazine* after he wrote critical things in his blog about *Times* editor Howell Raines.[6]

If there is disagreement over politics and policy among these bloggers, it is not because they come from radically divergent backgrounds. All of the top bloggers are white; Moulitsas, who is half Greek and half Latino, is

---

[5] While it is unclear whether Drum considers himself a journalist, there is no question that he currently is employed by a traditional media organization.

[6] As of this writing, Sullivan has been hired by the *Atlantic Monthly*, and has moved his blog on to its Web site.

the only arguable exception. Neither is the picture of gender diversity an inspiring one. At the time the survey was conducted, Cox was the only woman among this group of top bloggers.

Yet perhaps the most striking characteristic of this group is its educational attainment. Of the top ten blogs, eight are run by people who have attended an elite institution of higher education—either an Ivy League school, or a school of similar caliber like Caltech, Stanford University, or the University of Chicago. Seven of the top ten are run by someone with a JD or a PhD—and one of the exceptions, Cox, did graduate work at Berkeley and worked as an editor at the *Chronicle of Higher Education*. At least three of the ten bloggers—Marshall, Reynolds, and Drum—are the children of academics.

All of this raises the question, How different are bloggers from what many bloggers derisively term the "elite media"? Like traditional journalism, blog traffic is concentrated on a small number of outlets. Many blogs are run by journalists or by those with journalistic training. And journalists or not, all of the top ten bloggers have advantages that distinguish them from ordinary citizens. Political consultants and Yale-educated lawyers have not traditionally been underrepresented in the corridors of political power. Even those with the least previous connection to journalism and politics— namely, Drum and Johnson—possess uncommon technical expertise and management experience. Business owners and executives, too, have not historically been an underrepresented class in U.S. politics.

Yet the relatively elite social background of the top ten bloggers is in itself not conclusive. Many of these bloggers dispute the claim that they represent a privileged set of citizens. Moulitsas, Hewitt, and Reynolds have all written books celebrating the power of the netroots—books with titles like *Crashing the Gates* or *An Army of Davids*. Bloggers often emphasize the community production of information in the blogosphere. It is common to talk about blogging as an ecosystem, in which both large and small blogs have their place. The ease with which blogs can link to one another, and the norms that require bloggers to acknowledge one another's work, mean in theory that anyone can point out insights that others have neglected.

The culture of blogging may somewhat ameliorate the elitism inherent in having blog readership focused on a few bloggers who are unrepresentative of the general public. Still, there are limits to what the openness of blogging culture can accomplish. The top bloggers may read more blogs than the average citizen, but their reading habits are likely also skewed toward popular blogs. It is one thing if the top ten bloggers, who serve as filters for the rest of the blogosphere, come from relatively elite backgrounds. But what of the second- and third-tier bloggers? If we are to take seriously the trickle up theory of online debate, we need to know who these ideas are trickling up from. We need systematic knowledge about a broader swath of the blogging community.

Blogger Census

To answer some of these questions, I conducted a census of top bloggers, combining publicly available biographical information with a short survey distributed via e-mail. Numerous postmortems of the 2004 election declared that this was the election cycle when blogs arrived as a political force. Using average traffic for early December 2004 as a baseline, I attempted to gather information on every political blog that averaged more than two thousand visitors a week.[7] The list was compiled from N.Z. Bear's Blogosphere Ecosystem project, which aggregated data from the SiteMeter tracking service. Eighty-seven political blogs had at least this level of traffic; I was able to gather detailed background information on seventy-five of these eighty-seven blog publishers.[8]

A census of political bloggers naturally raises questions of scale. It makes sense to focus on the top part of the power-law curve, the sites that get the majority of the blog traffic, but deciding how far down to delve in the blog rankings is a matter of judgment. The cutoff of two thousand visitors a day was chosen for both theoretical and practical reasons. From the perspective of mass politics, two thousand daily visitors seemed to be beyond the point of diminishing returns. Choosing a different cutoff—say, one thousand readers per day—would have doubled the number of bloggers to be surveyed, yet together the added blogs would have had fewer

---

[7] The hope was that a month following the election, the traffic numbers would be closer to normal levels. For those blogs that received greater exposure during the run-up to the election, the December 2004 data also provided an indication of whether increased exposure had translated into higher average readership.

[8] The blogs tracked by the Bear Blog Ecosystem project that did not focus on politics were excluded from the analysis.

readers than DailyKos or Instapundit. Limiting the census to eighty-seven blogs also allowed the survey to be conducted by a single researcher.

Because blog traffic is not fixed, this survey should be seen as a representative snapshot of a moving target. Many short-term factors, such as a link from a more prominent blog, can influence a blog's traffic on a given day or week. Looking at these blogs a few weeks later might therefore have generated a slightly different set of sites in the sample, particularly for blogs near the two-thousand-visitor cutoff.

Information on these top bloggers was collected in two ways. First, an attempt was made to find out about bloggers' backgrounds through public sources—news articles found through Lexis-Nexis, Google searches on the individual's name, and biographies or curriculum vitae posted by bloggers themselves. For the top ten bloggers, for example, all information was gathered through public sources. When public information was not available, bloggers were sent e-mails asking them to take a short survey focusing on their social background, education, and occupational history.

The fact that this survey was able to be conducted at all shows that bloggers are an accessible bunch. The large majority of them were polite, friendly, and eager to respond to the queries of a social scientist. This fact is particularly remarkable given the massive volume of e-mail that most of these individuals receive.

Unlike any other area of political discourse, it is common for bloggers to write under pseudonyms or just their first names. Of the eighty-seven blogs included in the study, twenty-four fell into that category. These pseudonymous bloggers were invited to take the survey, but were encouraged to withhold or be vague about details that might prove personally identifying. Of the ten active bloggers who failed to respond to our entreaties, only two blog under their real names.[9]

Twenty-five blogs from the total sample contained regular postings from more than one blogger. The nature of these arrangements varied significantly, from two friends who collaborated in producing the site, to a loosely affiliated group of ten or more contributors. For blogs with multiple

---

[9] In addition to these ten, two of the blogs included in the original eighty-seven sites stopped updating their content during the weeks the survey was conducted. Neither of these bloggers responded to our queries.

posters, the individual responsible for the largest number of posts was asked to take the survey.

With data gathered on seventy-five of the eighty-seven bloggers, the response rate for the survey greatly exceeds the average, though this includes many about whom information was gathered from public sources. Nevertheless, eight of the twenty-four pseudonymous bloggers—one-third of the total—failed to fill out the survey. This is the category of blogger about which I can say the least.

Education

If the A-list bloggers profiled above share remarkable educational pedigrees, the wider group of bloggers in our census does too. First, all but two of the respondents had graduated from college. This is, of course, well above the average in the general population. Even more revealing is the quality of the undergraduate and graduate institutions these bloggers attended. The survey asked bloggers to name any institutions they had attended for college and graduate school. From these data, I determined whether bloggers had attended an elite educational institution at some point in their academic careers. Elite educational institutions were defined as:

1. Institutions ranked in the top thirty by the 2004 *U.S. News and World Report* survey of universities. This group includes all seven Ivy League universities, many other prestigious private universities, and several prominent public research institutions. Non–Ivy League examples from the sample include Stanford University, the University of Chicago, Rice University, Emory University, the University of Michigan, and the University of California at Berkeley.
2. Highly selective liberal arts colleges, defined as one of the top twenty liberal arts colleges in the 2004 *U.S. News and World Report* rankings. Examples from the sample include Williams College, Swarthmore College, and Claremont McKenna College.
3. The U.S. military service academies, including the U.S. Military Academy at West Point, the U.S. Naval Academy at Annapolis, and the U.S. Air Force Academy, plus the graduate school at the Command and General Staff College.

Of the sixty-seven respondents who named the colleges or universities that they had attended, forty-three—nearly two-thirds—had attended at least one elite institution.[10] A strong majority of these bloggers also held an advanced degree. Forty-six of the seventy-five bloggers—61 percent—had earned a master's or a doctorate. (According to the Census Bureau's 2002 Current Population Survey, 9 percent of U.S. adults held an advanced degree.) Fifty-five out of the seventy-five respondents fell into at least one of these two categories.

That is not all. There are roughly 1 million lawyers in the United States, out of an adult population of 217 million (Ayres 2005). Yet lawyers or those with a JD make up 20 percent of the top bloggers, comprising fifteen out of the seventy-five respondents. Similar findings hold true for PhDs and professors. Twelve of the top bloggers have PhDs or MDs—16 percent of the total. Nineteen bloggers, more than a quarter of the sample, are current or former professors. Seven of these nineteen are law professors, making legal scholars especially prominent online.

These findings look even more dramatic when educational background is weighted by readership. Two-thirds of the traffic in our sample went to bloggers with a doctorate—a JD, PhD, or MD. No other segment of the media drives such a large portion of its audience to such highly educated individuals.

Bloggers have often been contrasted (negatively) with traditional journalists. Yet how do these groups really compare? One metric comes from a 1996 study by the American Society of Newspaper Editors. According to the American Society of Newspaper Editors (1997), only 90 percent of newspaper journalists have a bachelor's degree, while only 18 percent of newspaper journalists have graduate degrees. It is probably unfair to place our small, elite group of bloggers alongside a broad, representative sample of newspaper journalists. But journalists still commonly compare the two groups, and blog traffic is far more concentrated on top bloggers than newspaper readership is on top journalists.

---

[10] The specific names of educational institutions attended are particularly likely to be personally identifying, and many pseudonymous bloggers chose not to reveal that information. In cases where these bloggers provided enough information to judge the caliber of the school that they attended—such as noting it was an Ivy League institution or a "standard state school"—they have been included in the results. Otherwise, these respondents have been omitted.

Occupation and Technical Background

The top bloggers have more education, from more prestigious schools, than do most journalists or most members of the public. Unsurprisingly, this group has also been highly successful in the workplace.

First, many bloggers are themselves journalists. Sixteen of the seventy-five bloggers in our sample, or 21 percent, have been either professional journalists, or regular writers for a newspaper or magazine. Yet this count understates the number of bloggers with journalistic experience. Fourteen additional bloggers reported close contact with journalism, such as public relations professionals who routinely write press releases, or bloggers who were college journalists or opinion columnists. Overall, nearly two-fifths claimed close familiarity with traditional reporting, periodical publishing, or opinion journalism.

Many bloggers who are neither lawyers, professors, or journalists work in the business world. For those who do come from the private sector, what kinds of jobs do they have? Most bloggers seem to be educational elites; are those in the business sector largely business elites?

The answer seems to be yes. The survey tried to measure the extent to which individuals had held senior corporate posts. It defined bloggers as business elites when they fell into at least one of four categories:

1. Those who have owned or served on the board of a business.
2. Those employed as a corporate officer at the rank of vice president or higher.
3. Those who have worked as a senior management consultant, either as an individual or an employee of a prestigious management consulting firm such as MacKinsey or the Boston Consulting Group.
4. Those who showed other evidence of serving in a senior strategic management role. (One example from the sample was a senior business professor, who had done work for several Fortune 500 companies.)

Thirty-seven percent of the sample—twenty-seven of seventy-three respondents—qualify as past or present business elites under these criteria. The private-sector voices heard in the blogosphere are not those of cubicle jockeys or service industry workers. They are overwhelming those of business owners, senior executives, and business consultants.

Lastly, many bloggers have professional expertise in computer systems. The survey looked at the number of respondents who had academic degrees in computer science or electrical engineering, who held or had held jobs that depended primarily on their expertise in technology (from engineering work to Web design to technical support), or who were technology journalists. Thirty out of seventy-five respondents—39 percent of the sample—fell into one of these three categories.

The unmistakable conclusion is that almost all the bloggers in the sample are elites of one sort or another. More than two-thirds were educational elites, holding either an advanced degree or having attended one of the nation's most prestigious schools. A hugely disproportionate number of bloggers are lawyers or professors. Many are members of the elite media that the blogosphere so often criticizes. An even larger fraction are business elites, those who are either business owners or corporate decision makers. Also hugely overrepresented in the blogosphere are technical elites, those who get paid to work with technology. In fact, in the sample, there is only one respondent who is neither a journalist, nor a technical, educational, or business elite.

These educational and occupational data suggest a broader point about the professional skills that bloggers possess. In a general, bloggers are people who write for a living. From professors to public relations specialists, from lawyers to lobbyists, from fiction authors to management consultants to technical writers, the large majority of bloggers depend on the written word for their livelihood. Running a successful political blog requires strong analytic training, an encyclopedic knowledge of politics, the technical skill necessary to set up and maintain a blog, and writing ability equal to that of a print journalist. It is not an accident that there are no factory workers or janitors in the upper ranks of the blogosphere.

There is another element, too, that favors those from professional backgrounds. Running a world-class blog requires both free time and autonomy over one's schedule. Jakob Nielsen (1999), a well-known usability expert, talks about "stickiness"—defined as the ability of a site to convert users who stumble across it into repeat visitors. According to Nielsen, the largest factor in a site's stickiness is how frequently the content is updated.

The top blogs are by definition the stickiest sites of their kind. Almost all are updated several times a day. The need to update frequently is a key part of the infrastructure of blogging, and this systematically reduces the readership of anyone with an incompatible occupation. No one working a ten-hour shift at Wendy's would be able to update her blog on a smoke break. Professors, lawyers, and business owners often have no direct supervisor, and no one to set their schedule. In the blogosphere, as in the Athenian agora, those who devote themselves to public debates are those with social autonomy.

Gender, Race, and Ethnicity

While nearly anyone can start a blog, the most widely read political bloggers are not average Joes. In several ways, that may be a good thing. The skill set required of top bloggers is extensive, and if the top blogs really were written by random members of the public, fewer people would read them.

Yet if bloggers are a remarkably successful and well-educated group, the data suggest other potential problems for democratic politics. First, few political blogs are run by women. In addition to Cox, who edits the blog Wonkette, the sample included only four other blogs with female proprietors. Jeralyn Merritt, fifty-five, is a nationally known criminal defense attorney who runs the crime blog TalkLeft.com. Ann Althouse, fifty-two, is a professor of law at the University of Wisconsin at Madison. Betsy Newmark, forty-seven, is a history and civics teacher from Raleigh, North Carolina. Finally, a blog called the Daily Recycler, which posted video clips of news events, listed its author as "Sally," a woman living in Seattle, Washington.[11] (Michelle Malkin, a prominent conservative syndicated columnist, would also have been included in this group had her blog been featured in the SiteMeter rankings.) These numbers are in stark contrast with traditional journalists. According to the American Society of Newspaper Editors (1997) survey, 37 percent of newspaper reporters are women; for reporters under thirty, the gender ratio is exactly even.

If the relative absence of women's voices in the blogosphere stands out from the survey data, the situation is at least as striking regarding racial and ethnic diversity. Consider the case of Oliver Willis. Willis, twenty-seven, is a centrist Democrat who lives in the Washington, DC, suburbs. At the time of our census, Willis worked in the Web department of Media Matters for America, a left-leaning media watchdog organization that also

---

[11] Sally did not respond to our e-mails, and seems to have stopped updating her Web site.

employed (in presumably more lavish style) the blogger Atrios, otherwise known as former economics professor Duncan Black. According to Bear's SiteMeter data, Willis was the only identifiably African American blogger to receive more than two thousand visitors a day. During the week this study was done, Willis averaged roughly four thousand daily visitors, or less than 2 percent of the traffic received by Daily Kos.

Other racial and ethnic minorities seem largely absent in the blogosphere. In addition to Willis and Moulitsas, one pseudonymous blogger identified himself as Asian. A Google search of his blog archives, looking for keywords related to this ethnicity, suggested that this part of his heritage was unknown to his readers. These are the only identifiable voices of color in our sample.

Bloggers and Op-Ed Columnists

Bloggers are often compared with traditional journalists; yet as we saw above, the most popular bloggers come from social and educational backgrounds far more elite than that of the typical newspaper journalist. If we want to understand how blogs are influencing public discourse, and how blogging is different from previous forms of commentary, newspaper reporters do not provide the best yardstick. A better measure comes from comparing our group of bloggers with the few dozen op-ed columnists who write for the nation's most prestigious newspapers.

Like op-ed columnists, bloggers are in the business of political argument and persuasion; with a few exceptions, bloggers do not routinely engage in reportage. The bloggers in our sample with traditional media experience are overwhelmingly opinion journalists. Increasingly, the audience that top blogs attract is comparable to that of opinion columnists in an elite newspaper. According to comScore MediaMetrix, NYTimes .com received 14.6 million unique visitors in October 2004, the month preceding the presidential election (New York Times Digital 2004). It has been claimed that Daily Kos received more than 8 million visitors per month over the same period—and as Moulitsas put it, "This isn't a newspaper. They're all coming to read me. Not the sports page" (quoted in Nevius 2004).

Op-ed columnists are highly public individuals, and without exception, detailed biographies are only a Google search away. For our purposes,

I looked at all columnists writing on at least a biweekly schedule for the *New York Times*, the *Wall Street Journal*, the *Washington Post*, and the *Los Angeles Times* as of January 10, 2005. The number of columnists and the frequency with which they write varies across the four papers. The *Los Angeles Times* had four op-ed columnists, while at the other extreme the *Washington Post* had a dozen regular op-ed writers; there were thirty writers across the four publications. These thirty columnists were compared against the top thirty bloggers about whom I was able to learn full background information.

These regular op-ed columnists are by definition the elite of the elite. By a significant majority, they are the product of elite educational institutions. Overwhelmingly, they are white men. Partly by virtue of their professional obligations, they live in major coastal urban centers. Yet these columnists as a group are in some ways more representative of the public than the top bloggers are. The columnists *are* somewhat more likely than the bloggers to have attended an Ivy League school. Fourteen of the columnists are Ivy Leaguers, compared to ten of the bloggers. This Ivy League gap is particularly pronounced at the undergraduate level. Eleven of the columnists received their undergraduate degree from the Ivy League, while "only" six of the top thirty bloggers can say the same.

But if we are willing to look beyond the Ivy League, and count schools like Stanford, Caltech, the University of California at Berkeley, and Swarthmore as elite institutions, all of the educational gaps are reversed. According to the standards used above—the nation's top thirty universities, along with the top twenty liberal arts colleges—it is the bloggers who have the advantage. Two-thirds of the op-ed columnists have attended at least one elite educational institution; 73 percent of the bloggers fall into the same category. Slightly less than half of the columnists have either an advanced graduate degree or have done graduate study, in contrast to 70 percent of the bloggers. Twenty percent of the op-ed columnists have earned a doctoral degree; more than half of the bloggers have done the same.

Bloggers also look remarkable compared to other elite groups in U.S. society. Consider Peter Cappelli and Monika Hamori's work on the educational backgrounds of executives holding "c-level" posts in Fortune 100 corporations—chief executive officer, chief financial officer, chief operating officer, and chief technology officer, as well as division heads and senior vice presidents. They found that 10 percent of these executives had a bachelor's degree from the Ivy League (Cappelli and Hamori 2004).

Across the sample of seventy-five, 16 percent of the bloggers had an undergraduate Ivy League degree.

These findings raise the question of what, exactly, the phrase elite media means. These top bloggers have educational backgrounds that exceed those of professional columnists. The readership of the top blogs rivals the nation's top op-ed pages. Moreover, the blogosphere has succeeded in re-creating some of the traditional punditocracy's most worrisome elitist characteristics.

One of these is a dearth of gender and ethnic diversity. Then *New York Times* op-ed columnist Anna Quindlen (2006) remarked in 1990 that most op-ed pages operated with a "quota of one" for female columnists. A decade and a half later, these facts had hardly changed. As of 2005 Maureen Dowd, who succeeded Quindlen, remained the only female op-ed writer on the *Times'* staff. The *Los Angeles Times* and the *Washington Post* also had one female columnist; the *Wall Street Journal* had two. That brought female representation on elite opinion pages to five out of thirty columnists. Blogs have not improved on this record, with only three female bloggers in the top thirty.

The same story holds true for racial and ethnic minorities. There are three African American op-ed columnists, but there are no identifiable African Americans among the top thirty bloggers. There was one Asian blogger, and one of mixed Latino heritage. Op-ed columnists may be a poor substantive representation of the U.S. public; yet in this regard it seems that top bloggers are even worse.

Rhetoric and Reality

Bloggers, like many political actors, often justify themselves by claiming to represent the viewpoints of ordinary citizens. Hewitt (2005) declares on the cover of his book *Blog* that "the blogosphere is smashing the old media monopoly and giving individuals power in the marketplace of ideas." Reynolds's (2005) book, *An Army of Davids*, is subtitled *How Markets and Technology Empower Ordinary People to Beat Big Media, Big Government, and Other Goliaths*. Jerome Armstrong and Moulitsas may disagree vehemently with Hewitt and Reynolds about politics, but their book *Crashing the Gates* also enthuses that blogging and the netroots enable "people-powered politics." Bloggers themselves have not been alone in making such claims. Newspapers and magazines have consistently alleged that blogging gives ordinary citizens greater influence on politics.

Some claims about blogs are true. Tens of millions of Americans now read political blogs at least occasionally; according to the Pew Internet and American Life Project, more than a million Americans have become political bloggers themselves. Blogs are not likely to replace traditional journalism, but blogging has already transformed the smaller niche of opinion journalism. The top blogs are now the most widely read sources of political commentary in the United States.

Yet the very success of the most popular bloggers undercuts blogging's central mythology. Of the perhaps one million citizens who write a political blog, only a few dozen have more readers than does a small-town newspaper. For every blogger who reaches a significant audience, ten thousand journal in obscurity. And while it is sometimes difficult to decide who counts as an ordinary citizen, the few dozen bloggers who get most of the blog readership are so *extra*ordinary that such debates are moot.

Rarely has the phrase the marketplace of ideas been so literal as with blogs. In order to be heard in the blogosphere, a citizen has to compete with millions of other voices. Those who come out on top in this struggle for eyeballs are not middle schoolers blogging about the trials of adolescence, nor are they a fictitious collection of pajama-clad amateurs taking on the old media from the comfort of their sofas. Overwhelmingly, they are well-educated white male professionals. Nearly all of the bloggers in our census were either educational elites, business elites, technical elites, or traditional journalists.

It is therefore difficult to conclude that blogging has changed which sorts of citizens have their voices heard in politics. If our primary concern is the factual accuracy of blogs or the quality of bloggers' analysis, the elite backgrounds of the top bloggers may be reassuring. Yet most Americans have not attended an elite university, and do not have an advanced degree. Most Americans are not journalists or computer professionals; most are not business owners, senior executives, or management consultants. Most Americans are not white men. The vigorous online debate that blogs provide may be, on balance, a good thing for U.S. democracy. But as many continue to celebrate the democratic nature of blogs, it is important to acknowledge that many voices are still left out.

Seven

Elite Politics and the "Missing Middle"

More tears are shed over answered prayers than
unanswered ones.

—Mother Theresa

Big changes in U.S. communications have rarely had immediate impacts on U.S. politics. Ten years passed between the release of the Mosaic browser and Dean's use of the Internet to break campaign fund-raising records. Significant numbers of U.S. households started buying televisions in 1949 and 1950; yet it was not until the Kennedy-Nixon debates a decade later that political scientists had clear evidence that television had changed presidential politics (Kelley 1962). The future influence of Franklin Delano Roosevelt's fireside chats was hardly obvious when radio was the province of teenage boys swapping music. From the beginning, there was a lively public debate over the benefits and costs of leaving the telegraph in private hands (Starr 2004). Still, few foresaw that a telegraph monopoly would lead to the Associated Press's news monopoly and its staggering influence on Gilded Age politics. The social and political dimensions of communications innovations have always matured more slowly than the technology itself.

This volume is thus a chronicle of the Internet in its adolescence. Many observers hurried to be the first to predict where the Internet would steer politics; it is much too late for this book to join that crowd. In the political realm the Internet has yet to reach full maturity; some methods of online campaigning remain experimental.

Yet while many details remain to be filled in, this book argues that the broad outlines of the Internet's political influence are already clear—and have been for some time. The patterns of inequality this book finds in political traffic have been documented in other parts of the Web for a decade. The Google search engine first went online in 1997. Many of the most important institutions and strategies of online politics are also far from novel. By the time this book is in print, MoveOn.org—which arguably remains the preeminent Internet-fueled advocacy group—will have celebrated its tenth anniversary (more about MoveOn below). The Internet is mature enough to be a core component of modern political campaigns. If the Web is indeed expanding the political voice of average citizens, then there should already be plenty of evidence to that effect.

In looking for the Internet's political impacts, one of the clearest historical lessons is the influence of infrastructure—broadly conceived—on the political possibilities of the medium. In the late 1920s and early 1930s, as radio emerged as a mass medium, political scientists focused almost exclusively on the technology needed to broadcast and receive radio waves. The name broadcasting itself implied that radio would be heard by a broad swath of the citizenry, allowing even the "unleavened mass of illiterates" to follow politics (Bromage 1930). The social breadth that radio required was assumed to be a good thing for democratic practice.

Yet a few years later, when the American Political Science Association's own civic education radio program was canceled by NBC, political scientists decided that their initial assessments had been too hasty. Their angry postmortems focused not on the technology itself but on the role of broadcast advertising, the relationship between the network and its affiliates, the funds needed to produce a successful radio program, and the rare personal qualities required of a radio personality (NACRE 1937). Abandoning his early enthusiasm, prominent political scientist Thomas Reed (1937) declared that these initially overlooked features transformed broadcasting into "a potential menace to culture and democracy."

For us, the lesson is largely the same. Just as with radio, political scientists have had an incomplete vision of what the infrastructure of the Internet includes. The TCP/IP protocol, which allows any computer on the Internet to talk to any other, is indeed remarkably open. The HTML used to create most Web content allows direct links to any online document.

In defining infrastructure, though, we should look beyond the simple technical details of the technology to the social, economic, political, and even cognitive processes that enable it. Even the cheapest hardware and the most open protocols do not eliminate inequalities in the creation of political content, or in finding that content once it is online. Academics as well as popular observers have too often focused just on the most open parts of the Internet architecture. In the process, our understanding of the Internet's political effects has been systematically distorted.

This is not to say that skepticism about the Internet's impact on U.S. democracy is new; in that regard this book has plenty of company. Other scholars have examined the digital divide, citizen interest (or disinterest) in politics, and the ability of established institutions—particularly news organizations, political parties, and interest groups—to move online. While all of those factors are important, this book has looked at a different set of concerns. In this concluding chapter, I want to begin by reiterating some of the barriers to political democratization that this book has emphasized. I then want to sketch, at least roughly, a narrative of online politics centered around what I term the missing middle.

The Limits of Online Politics

Low Levels of Politically Relevant Traffic

Political traffic is a tiny portion of Web usage. Traffic to political Web sites is sparser even than many skeptics have expected. Noncommercial sources of political information have failed to mount a real challenge to traditional media outlets, getting only a small fraction of the visitors that news and media sites receive. Traffic to political sites looks more paltry still when compared to other types of Web usage. According to Hitwise, pornographic content receives roughly one hundred times the traffic that political Web sites do.

If citizens, collectively, consume little political content, this has far-reaching consequences. Fewer eyeballs mean fewer resources, and also raise questions about how public the "networked public sphere" actually is.

Link Structure and Site Visibility

The link structure of the Web limits the content that citizens see. When Tim Berners-Lee created the first HTML pages, it was the ability of Internet documents to link to one another that was the great innovation. Links do not just provide paths for surfers; with the advent of Google, the number of links pointing to a site became a critical means by which search engines found and ranked content.

If links help determine online visibility, how links are distributed tells us much about who gets heard on the Web. This book shows that global patterns are repeated within political content. The Web is fractally organized, with winners-take-all patterns emerging at every level. The importance of links challenges notions that online equality is easy or inevitable.

Search Engines and Search Behavior

Much search engine use is shallow. Not only is the aggregate level of political interest low, the search strategies that citizens employ limit the political content they see. Part of the issue is the difference between navigational queries (which seek a specific site or online outlet) and content queries (which seek information on political topics or political personalities). In large part, citizens use search engines to seek out familiar sites and sources.

Navigational searches generate near-perfect agreement between Google and Yahoo!, the two top search engines. Yet even for queries that do not seek a specific information source, the overlap between search engines is high. If users favor simple search queries and then click only on the first few results returned, most of the political content indexed by search engines is irrelevant.

The Economics of Content Production

Even in the digital world, some content is expensive to produce. It may be cheap to start a blog—Web users can even have their blog hosted for free by companies like Blogger, LiveJournal, or MySpace—but it is a mistake to conflate blogs or small-scale political advocacy Web sites with traditional journalism. Even online, traditional news organizations supply most of the public's political news and information.

Blanket claims that the Internet is lowering barriers to entry are thus misleading. Many online firms face the same economic pressures that have created "natural" monopolies in numerous industries. Companies like Google and Yahoo! spend more of their revenue on equipment than a typical telephone company—and then they spend billions more in research and development.

Media companies have long tended toward concentration for the same reasons. When the Internet lowers the cost of distributing expensive-to-create content, it doesn't reverse the economic logic of concentration—it amplifies it. If additional readers require minimal extra cost, the Internet guarantees large economies of scale. We should be unsurprised when markets for political news and information show the same levels of concentration seen in other online markets.

Online Social Elites

Even in areas without incumbent players and where content is cheap for a single individual to produce, social hierarchies have quickly emerged. Again and again, we have heard claims that the Internet is shifting power away from political elites. The Internet is supposed to allow more voices to reach a nontrivial audience, and these new voices are supposed to be more representative of the general public.

Political blogs are perhaps the most important test of these claims; blogs may reach only a fraction of the public, but they are now the most widely read form of U.S. political commentary. While the tail of the distribution includes many hundreds of thousands of political bloggers, a small group of A-list bloggers actually gets more political blog traffic than *the rest of the citizenry combined.* Talk about blogs empowering ordinary citizens rings doubly hollow when the top bloggers are better educated, more frequently male, and less ethnically diverse than the elite media that blogs often criticize.

A Narrower Net

There are thus many reasons why online politics has proved less open than many expected. Sorting out the relative importance of these factors (including factors that other scholars have pointed to) is a question that still calls for future research. Yet what is indisputable is that the Internet has not led to a simple, wholesale shift from a few big outlets to lots of little ones. Small-scale, citizen-produced content is online, as hordes of political bloggers demonstrate. Still, the audience for online news outlets and political Web sites is shaped by two powerful and countervailing trends: continued or accelerated concentration among the most popular outlets, combined with fragmentation among the least-read ones. In nearly every online niche, we see attention accruing overwhelmingly to two categories of sites: a small set of winners that receive the lion's share of the traffic, and a host of tiny Web sites that, collectively, receive most of the remaining visitors. I have labeled this phenomenon the missing middle. I would suggest that this sharp divide between the biggest and smallest outlets is at the heart of many puzzling contradictions in Internet politics.

Much fuss continues to be made about small-scale information producers on the Web. This debate has taken many guises, from early discussions about narrowcasting or pointcasting, to talk about "the Daily Me" and personalized content, to more recent enthusiasm for the long tail. Benkler's defense of the "networked public sphere" (which I will return to below) follows in this same vein, arguing that the contributions of myriad small online information producers is transforming politics for the better. Even Sunstein's recent book *Infotopia* (2006)—in some ways a reversal from his earlier work—suggests that new, self-correcting aggregation techniques allow vast numbers of small information producers to contribute to public life. Talk by prominent bloggers about an "Army of Davids," an "Information Reformation," or how ordinary citizens are using the Internet to "crash the gates" follows much the same logic.

This focus on small content producers is partly deserved; as a group, such outlets *do* receive more of the total audience online than in traditional media. There are even well-known cases (though few and suspiciously overused) where little-trafficked Web sites seem to have triggered a "cybercascade," bringing facts or issues to wide attention.

But talk about small-scale online content has also been deeply misleading. Instead of the "inevitable" fragmentation of online media, audiences on the Web are actually *more* concentrated on the top ten or twenty outlets than are traditional media like newspapers and magazines. As chapter 5 suggested, the Internet is not a media Robin Hood, robbing from the audience rich and giving to the audience poor. In reality, it is middle-class outlets that have suffered the greatest relative decline in readership.

This bifurcation of online audiences toward both the most and least read outlets needs to be more widely understood, particularly in the context of online politics. We have seen the missing middle at every level of the Web, or at least in every place this book has looked: in overall Web traffic, visits to news and media sites, political Web traffic, the link structure of political advocacy communities, and even subcommunities of Web sites on one side of a political controversy or another. The problem with Anderson and others is that they have distorted the scale of the phenomenon they are examining; they have made the long tail into the entire dog. At least for news and media sites as well as political sites, it is simply not true that the smallest outlets, taken together, get most of the traffic. Not even close.

The Online Public Sphere

The political consequences of the missing middle are multifaceted, but perhaps nowhere are they clearer than with regard to the online public sphere. This book has been particularly critical of what it has referred to as trickle-up theories of online discourse. In these accounts, the social hierarchies that dominate blogging and other forms of online organizing are an essential and benign part of community-based production. Traffic over the entire Web might be highly concentrated, but smaller political niches are supposed to follow far more egalitarian patterns. Elite bloggers are believed to aggregate small contributions into a representative and useful whole; highly visible blogs filter the vast expanse of online opinion, while the (supposedly) larger number of gatekeepers provide myriad paths for ordinary citizens to inject concerns into public debate. Search engines such as Google ostensibly make even the most obscure content available to those motivated enough to search for it.

The missing middle suggests that such trickle-up theories rest on dubious assumptions. Proponents of the online public sphere typically insist that Internet content should be evaluated against the baseline of traditional media—but don't acknowledge that online audiences are just as concentrated on top outlets as audiences for print media are. Blogging may now be the most widely read form of political commentary, but (as I noted above) the bloggers in our census are grossly unrepresentative of the broader public. While Google and Yahoo! index billions of online documents, the design of search engines, the structure of the Web, and the shallowness of citizens' search strategies limit the "shelf space" available for any particular political topic.

Trickle-up theories of online politics also rely explicitly on a broad, representative set of moderate-size outlets that allow "vastly greater" numbers of citizens to find an audience (Benkler 2006, 242). It is not exactly clear what qualifies an outlet as "moderately read," nor how many midsize outlets are enough to satisfy the key role that Benkler and others assign them. But the power-law distribution of links and traffic is so extreme that no post hoc definition of moderately read can be satisfied. Moderately read outlets are precisely what the Web does *not* provide.

Benkler also claims that the tendency of Web sites to cluster in topical communities ameliorates the broader pattern of concentration, arguing that as we look at smaller niches and subniches of Web sites, "the obscurity of sites participating in the cluster diminishes" (2006, 248). This book has maintained that such conclusions hide a common but critical misunderstanding. The missing middle is not something that one can escape just by looking further down the rankings, or by dividing the Web into smaller and smaller categories of sites. It is true that different categories of content show somewhat different levels of audience concentration. Yet much computer science research has revealed that the Web displays self-similarity (see, for example, Song, Havlin, and Makse 2005; Dill et al. 2002). In a fractally organized Web, the winners-take-all patterns of the parts are mirrored in the winners-take-all pattern of the whole. After all, the power-law distribution of traffic that we see over the entire Web is just the sum of the traffic across all of the Web's component communities. A few categories of Web sites might diverge from the concentration seen in the overall Web traffic, but there is overwhelming evidence that political Web sites do not.

Scandals

Still, the biggest concern with networked theories of democracy is not that they are mistaken but that they do not acknowledge the trade-offs that are the price of the Internet's political successes. Though this book has been descriptive rather than normative in focus, it is clear that the Internet is strengthening some democratic values at the expense of others. The power-law structure of networked politics seems particularly well suited to a "fire alarm" or "burglar alarm" model of public oversight (Mccubbins and Schwartz 1984; Schudson 1999; Arnold 1990; J. Snider 2001; Zaller 2003; but see also Bennett 2003a.[1] Even the countless bloggers with few readers

---

[1] On this point, see the discussion in Bimber 1998; J. Snider 1996. As Bimber describes the argument, "The Net might increase the popular accountability of government without measurably enhancing the level of information or knowledge of individual voters" (143).

can get national attention if they uncover information that news organizations or elite bloggers find especially valuable or scandalous. Highly focused blog readership keeps the public's attention on a few, credible gatekeepers that can sound the alarm when policymakers stray too far from the preferences of the public. So long as large, national news organizations remain strong, the blogosphere may prove a valuable supplement to traditional outlets, filtering political information through a different set of constraints, concerns, and biases.

The Internet's clearest political impacts, then, come from the scandals that it has exposed, or at least allowed to unfold more rapidly. Yet many have hoped that the online public sphere would do more than just air dirty laundry. Scandals do not constitute the sort of moral discussion that some theorists take to be a central justification for deliberation (see, for example, Gutmann and Thompson 1996). For one thing, they do not typically involve areas of tough moral disagreement. There was little debate about whether Representative Mark Foley should have been sexually propositioning underage House pages. No one thought that CBS News should base its reporting on forged documents. Partisans and pundits may have disagreed about what Lott meant in his remarks at Thurmond's birthday party, but both sides loudly repudiated the segregationist ideals that underpinned Thurmond's 1948 campaign. Scandals are powerful political moments, in short, because they accuse public figures of doing things that citizens already agree are unacceptable.

Scandals are thus unusual. They represent extremely high-value political information, appeal to widely shared political values, and are usually easy to understand. Most of the time scandals serve the interests of one set of partisans or another. All of these characteristics make scandals exceptionally transmissible within networks. We should therefore expect scandals to be one place where the breathtakingly wide net cast by the long tail actually matters.

But although a few obscure bloggers have drawn attention to previously unknown political scandals, this does not necessarily mean that traditional outsiders have an easier time getting heard online. Top bloggers can command sustained, widespread attention to their views and preferences, while other bloggers need the cooperation of widely read outlets to be heard at all. The preferences of smaller bloggers are likely to be repeated and amplified when they fit with the views of elite outlets—otherwise, they are likely to be ignored.

The profile of those who have succeeded in touching off scandals reinforces the sense that it is elites who have been most successful at taking advantage of the Internet. "Buckhead," the anonymous Free Republic poster who claimed that CBS News was using forged documents, turned out to be longtime GOP figure Harry MacDougald, the prominent Atlanta lawyer who led the effort to disbar then-president Bill Clinton (Wallsten 2004a). The initially anonymous blogger who published Rep. Foley's "overly friendly" e-mails to former pages turned out to be Lane Hudson, a staffer for the Human Rights Campaign, the largest gay and lesbian advocacy group (Levey 2006). In these prominent cases, the Internet did not empower ordinary citizens; rather, it allowed disgruntled elites to get around institutional constraints.

"Middle Democracy" and the Missing Middle

From the perspective of deliberative democracy, the missing middle raises additional concerns. As we have seen, some have hoped that the public sphere in cyberspace would be a bit closer to a Habermasian ideal—that political discourse would be freer from corporate influences, and that public debates would be both more inclusive and more thoughtful. Yet as Andrew Chadwick (2006, 102) puts it, "The road to e-democracy is littered with the burnt-out hulks of failed projects." The online deliberation that *is* taking place has often been roundly criticized, even by some initial enthusiasts. Some have concluded that the design of online spaces favors consumers over citizens, and corporate interests over the public interest (Lessig 1999, 69; Mclaine 2003; Gamson 2003). Online discussions seem to have difficulty generating the mutual respect that democratic deliberation requires, particularly given the widespread "trolling" and "flaming" in online forums (see, for example, Kayany 1998; Herring 2002; Wilhelm 2000). Others have similarly worried that online "echo chambers" will promote polarization rather than compromise (Sunstein 2001; Shapiro 1999). And of course, political bloggers have been repeatedly attacked in the press for their supposedly uncivic practices.

But if online debate has not achieved "true" deliberation, it has given new urgency to the fears of deliberative democracy's skeptics. Lynn Sanders argues that deliberative democracy fails because "some citizens are better than others at articulating their views in rational, reasonable terms"; those whose voices go unheard "are likely to be those who are already underrepresented in formal political institutions and who are systematically materially disadvantaged, namely women; racial minorities, especially Blacks; and poorer people" (1997; 348, 349) Peter Berkowitz (1996) concludes that deliberation empowers an even narrower set of citizens:

> Since it shifts power from the people to the best deliberators
> among them, deliberative democracy . . . appears to be in effect an
> aristocracy of intellectuals. In practice, power is likely to flow
> to the deans and directors, the professors and pundits, and all
> those who, by virtue of advanced education, quickness of thought,
> and fluency of speech can persuade others of their prowess in
> the high deliberative arts.

Something very much like Berkowitz's vision has already taken hold online. The online public sphere is already a de facto aristocracy dominated by those skilled in the high deliberative arts.

Political Organizing and the Missing Middle

If the vision of the online public sphere presented in this book is dispiriting to deliberative democrats, there are other ways, too, in which online politics raises new concerns. Paradoxically, expanded political participation has also brought an expanded role for political elites. By concentrating audiences, the barriers discussed above increase the influence of those running the top outlets. Activities such as political fund-raising or campaign volunteer work may be becoming more inclusive, but even here it is difficult to conclude that the power of political elites has simply diminished.

The Internet seems to be good at gathering large, loose, geographically dispersed groups together to pursue common goals. Through technologies like Meetup.com, Dean was able to create local volunteer organizations from diffuse nationwide interest. Dean broke fund-raising records by relying on tens of thousands of small online donors, not a handful of large contributors. From the Seattle WTO protests to the Million Mom March, other scholars have also concluded that networked politics is changing the logic of collective action, and increasingly favoring broad, diffuse interests (Bennett 2003b; Bimber 2003a; Lupia and Sin 2003; Postmes and Brunsting 2002).

Another prominent example in this vein is MoveOn.org, online organizing's best-known Cinderella story. MoveOn.org was founded largely accidentally in 1998 by Wes Boyd and Joan Blades, two software entrepreneurs. Boyd and Blades created an online petition calling on Congress to halt the impeachment of President Clinton, and instead to "censure and move on." An e-mail that Boyd and Blades sent to less than one hundred friends and acquaintances spread rapidly, and their online petition ultimately gathered more than five hundred thousand signatures. The e-mail list, Web site, and social networks assembled in the anti-impeachment campaign served as the core for future efforts.

By any standard, MoveOn.org has been a remarkable organizational success. MoveOn's Web site claims that the organization has more than three million members. According to the Center for Responsive Politics, MoveOn.org's 527 political organization disbursed $20 million during the 2004 calendar year, ranking it eighth among all advocacy groups. Yet in one respect, this success story suggests that online politics is shallower than it appears. MoveOn.org is by far the most successful organization of its type; at the moment, it is difficult to imagine any other online advocacy group raising nearly a million dollars in a weekend, as MoveOn has done (Whittington 2005). As we saw in chapter 3, there are thousands of small-scale advocacy groups online; however, most evidence of the Internet's political impact comes from a handful of large organizations.

The examples of the Dean campaign and MoveOn, patterns of links and traffic among advocacy sites, and early evidence from the Obama campaign all suggest that the missing middle applies to online organizing, too. MoveOn dominates its political niche much like Amazon.com dominates online bookselling or eBay dominates online auctions. There have been persistent attempts over the past decade to duplicate the MoveOn phenomenon (see, for example, Allen 2007). Many of these have been well-funded efforts involving prominent public figures and seasoned political staffers. But none has mobilized anything like MoveOn's corps of activists.

Given the mythology that still surrounds online politics, it is necessary to emphasize the obvious. The small group of bloggers who receive tens of thousands of hits daily are clearly political elites. Prominent online political groups, such as MoveOn.org, still rely heavily on formal and informal elites to run their organizations. Political candidates and their paid staff members *certainly* qualify as political elites. All of the most celebrated examples of online politics have relied on political elites in order to persuade, coordinate, and organize. Moreover, the new Internet elites are not necessarily more representative of the general public than the old elites are. Those claiming that the Internet is democratizing politics need to start by acknowledging these central facts.

New Technology, Old Failures

Before this book concludes, it is worth remarking on another, older school of scholarship that also seems to have something to say about the Internet's successes and failures. At least since the 1950s, political scientists have relied primarily on theories of pluralism to explain the distribution of power within U.S. politics. Pluralists describe policymaking as a negotiation among interest groups and public officials, with different sets of competing elites ascendant in different policy arenas. Pluralists argue that political resources are unequal but "noncumulative"—that most citizens have some power resources, and no one type of political resource (particularly wealth) eclipses all the rest. Because there are multiple centers of power in political decision making, and because the political system provides multiple opportunities to shape policy, pluralists have contended that U.S. democracy prevents one group or class of citizens from consistently dominating.

Yet as Schattschneider's epigraph for the previous chapter suggests, pluralism has never lacked for critics, even amid its own ranks. The central criticisms have been remarkably consistent over the past half century—namely, that U.S. democracy fails to provide adequate representation across lines of race and class, and that it fails to bridge the gap between policy elites and the mass public.

If these really are the most pressing problems with U.S. pluralism, thus far it is hard to conclude that the Internet has solved them. There are, of course, many areas of politics where the Internet's long-term impact remains hazy. But with political blogs, political entrepreneurs such as MoveOn's Boyd and Blades, and even widely known incidents such as "Rathergate" and the Foley scandal, those whose political voices have been amplified the most have been white, upper-middle-class, highly educated professionals. In the areas where the evidence is the clearest, the Internet seems like the answer to a problem that U.S. politics did not have.

The persistence of the digital divide makes the failures of pluralism and online deliberation even more salient. A decade of scholarship has documented continuing inequalities in access to the Internet, the skills required to find and process online content, and the desire to seek out political information on the Web. But if it takes substantial skill and motivation to *read* political blogs, this book has shown that the skills and commitment necessary to *be read* online are several orders of magnitude more exclusive.

Ultimately, then, the Internet seems to be both good news and bad news for the political voice of the average citizen. The Internet has made campaign financing more inclusive, and allowed broad, diffuse interests to organize more easily. For motivated citizens, vast quantities of political information are only a click away. Internet politics is not just politics as usual; online interests are hardly a perfect reflection of the off-line political landscape.

Yet where the Internet has failed to live up to its billing has to do with the most direct kind of political voice. If we consider the ability of ordinary citizens to write things that other people will see, the Internet has fallen far short of the claims that continue to be made about it. It may be easy to speak in cyberspace, but it remains difficult to be heard.

Appendix

On Data and Methodology

Support Vector Machine Classifiers

For social scientists attempting to do a systematic study of the Internet, the size of the Web is a central problem. As of this writing, Google claims to index more than eight billion online documents. A researcher could spend an entire lifetime online and still see only a minuscule fraction of the total content posted on the World Wide Web. How, then, can we gather accurate data about the broad expanse of online materials available to citizens?

One response is to use technological solutions to this technological problem. There are a variety of different automated techniques for cataloging, categorizing, and classifying Web pages and other online documents. For the portion of my research described in chapter 3, my research partners and I relied on SVM classifiers. With the assistance of NEC Research Labs—and particularly NEC researchers Kostas Tsioutsiouliklis and Judy A. Johnson—SVM methods were used to classify Web pages. In this case, hundreds of thousands of HTML documents were downloaded using Web crawlers. We wanted a way to determine which pages were relevant to the topics we were interested in—for example, which of these thousands of pages dealt with the issue of abortion, and which did not.

This appendix seeks to outline and clarify the methodology we used. It attempts to explain the basics of what SVMs are, how they work in practice, and what issues other scholars should bear in mind as they assess this research. While the emphasis here is on praxis rather than theory, references are provided to in-depth articles and books on the rapidly evolving literature on SVMs.

There are several basic facts about SVMs that must be understood before discussing the mathematics behind them. First of all, SVMs are a method of supervised machine learning—a way of creating a function from training data. The SVM is fed a series of objects with the "correct" values assigned by a human operator. The SVM looks at the "features" of the objects, and based these training examples, creates a function that assigns differential weight to these different features. In theory, then, the SVM learns inductively which features of an object are important, and which are not.

Second, SVMs can be used to assign either continuous values ("regression") or discrete values ("classification"). We are concerned with the use of SVMs as classifiers. In this role, it is important to understand that SVMs are binary classifiers. They provide a yes or no answer, separating cases into one of two groups—a positive set, and a negative set. While SVMs can be assigned more complex classification tasks, this requires breaking down the learning tasks into a binary branching tree, and in essence training one SVM for every branch point. To understand how this branching tree might work in practice, consider one task that SVMs have proved good at: recognizing handwritten characters. One might train SVMs, first, to classify a handwritten character as either uppercase or lowercase; at the lowest level of the tree, it may be asked to distinguish between similar characters such as g and q.

SVMs use a hyperplane to separate the training data into two classes, trying in the process to maximize the margin—that is, to make the distance from the closest examples of the two different types as large as possible. Each case, or piece of the data, is represented as a single point in a high-dimensional space. Once the training set is used to draw the hyperplane, new data points are classified by which side of the hyperplane they are on. This process may sound complicated, but as I explain below, the intuition behind it is easy to understand.

To see how this is so, consider figure A.1. It shows a simple SVM in action. Real SVMs draw decision boundaries in thousands or hundreds of thousands of dimensions; figure A.1 asks us to draw a decision boundary in only two dimensions. In this figure, we can see two different types of

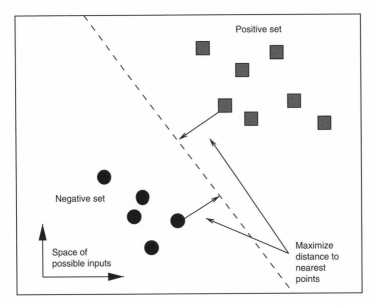

Figure A.1
This figure shows a simple linear SVM. The boundary decision line is drawn to maximize the distance between itself and the *support vectors*, which are defined by the points closest to the line. This example owes much to the explication of Platt 1998.

data points: circles and squares. The circles and squares are placed on the plot by their values on two sample covariates: their values of X, and their values of Y. The squares tend to have high values of both X and Y; the circles tend to have low values on both of these variables. Consequently, the circles are clustered in the lower left-hand corner of the plot, and the squares are grouped in the upper right corner.

These two groups of points are the "training set"—the initial set of points that teach the SVM where to draw the boundary separating the two groups. The next question is how exactly to draw this boundary. SVMs work in a manner that may at first be counterintuitive to social scientists used to techniques like ordinary least squares regression: they ignore most of the data. The key process, again, is to maximize the margin: to identify the small set of points closest to a boundary line that can cleanly separate the two groups. In figure A.1, points in the top right or lower left of the graph are not near the margin, and therefore have no influence on drawing the decision boundary. Now consider only the points closest to the boundary line, marked on the graph with arrows. The boundary line is drawn to put the greatest possible distance between the decision boundary and these points at the margins.

Once the boundary line is drawn, classification is simple. The SVM can be presented with new data points, where only these points' values of X and Y are known. If these points are above the line, they are classified as squares; if they are below the line, they are classified as circles.

If we extrapolate this example to larger numbers of dimensions, we get a fair approximation of how SVMs function. If we have three dimensions instead of the two in our example, a plane rather than a line is required to draw the decision boundary. In four or more dimensions, a hyperplane is required. Formally, a hyperplane is an N-dimensional analogue of a plane; it serves to divide an $N + 1$ dimensional space into two parts.

This simple example raises a few obvious questions. First of all, what if it isn't possible to separate the two groups cleanly? In many real-world data sets, there may not be a single hyperplane that can split the positive and negative sets. Corinna Cortes and Vladimir Vapnik (1995) introduced what they termed a "soft margin" method to deal with cases of mislabeled examples. This refinement was a significant advance over Vapnik's original formulation. Soft margin algorithms choose a hyperplane that provides the maximum margin for the nearest cleanly split examples, effectively disregarding those data points on the "wrong" side of the boundary.

If SVMs work by drawing hyperplane decision boundaries in high-dimensional spaces, it is important to understand how the objects to be classified are mapped onto this space. The methods of mapping vary greatly depending on the context and application. But in our case, they are relatively straightforward. As I noted above, we are interested in classifying text documents—specifically, large numbers of Web pages written in HTML. In each of the dozen Web communities we examine, the training set consists of two hundred Web pages focused on a political topic, and several thousand pages of random Web content.

Each of these Web pages in the training set is treated as an object; the next task is determining what "features" these objects have that allow the two hundred relevant pages to be distinguished from the random content. We begin by discarding any HTML formatting. Punctuation and stop words—such as "the"—are also removed. Then, we compile a list of *all* words and word pairs contained in the training set. This list is large—in our examples, the total number of words or word pairs is in the low hundreds of thousands.

Each of these words and word pairs then becomes a "feature." If there are 120,000 different words or word pairs in the training set pages, for instance, then *each* Web page has 120,000 different features. For each feature, every Web page is given one of only two values: a "1" if the Web page contains at least one instance of that word or pair of words, or a "0" if it does not. (This 1 or 0 coding scheme is a matter of computational convenience; one could also count the number of times the word appears, or adopt some other scheme based on ordered categories. The experiences of Tsioutsiouliklis and Johnson, however, have led them to the opinion that more detailed coding makes little difference to the actual categorization.)

The next step is to map each of these Web pages as a single point in a large dimensional space. Each feature becomes a single dimension; if the the number of features identified is 120,000, for example, then the space has 120,000 dimensions. The point in this space corresponding to each Web page is identified by its value—in this case, either 1 or 0—on each dimension.

Drawing a decision boundary in two dimensions is easy; computing the maximum margin boundary in a space with thousands of points and hundreds of thousands of dimensions is much less trivial. In particular, drawing the margin requires solving a difficult quadratic programming optimization problem. For the purposes of this book, sequential minimal optimization is used (Platt 1998). Introduced by John Platt, this technique makes training an SVM significantly less computationally intensive.

Once this decision boundary is drawn, the SVM is considered to be "trained." Newly encountered Web pages can be classified by their position in this space. HTML formatting and stop words in these pages are again discarded; so are words and word pairs not in the training set. Once the hyperplane is drawn, classification is rapid. As chapter 3 explains, in order to be slightly more cautious, we actually divide the sites into three rather than two categories. Positive sites are those significantly above the hyperplane; sites significantly below the margin are classified as negative. Sites about which the SVM was unsure—that is, sites that are quite close to the decision boundary—are classified as "unsure."

Advantages and Disadvantages of SVM Classification

The above section should serve as a basic introduction to how SVMs function and the methodology we followed in employing them. Just as important, however, is a discussion of why this technique is attractive in our case, and what potential disadvantages it may possess.

SVM techniques have received a good deal of attention from computer scientists and learning theorists in recent years, and have found uses in a wide variety of applications—from face detection (Osuna, Freund, and Girosi 1997) to handwritten character recognition (LeCun et al. 1995). They have proven particularly effective in classifying content based on text features—an area where SVM methods show substantial performance improvements over the previous state of the art, while at the same time proving to be more robust (Joachims 1998). All of these are complex tasks that are relatively easy for human beings to accomplish, but that have been traditionally difficult for computers.

The areas where SVMs have been successful, then, highlight the potential advantages of this technique. First of all, SVMs allow decisions to be made based on an extremely large number of potential factors, even when these factors cannot be systematically identified *ex ante*. Cognitive scientists, for example, cannot provide a simple or easily defined set of rules about how human beings recognize handwritten characters. Nonetheless, with a large training set, SVMs can learn to make the "correct" classification of the character the large majority of the time, based on complex criterion that human coders cannot themselves articulate.

Second, SVM techniques are highly scalable. In our case, it was literally impossible for human coders to classify the millions of Web pages we downloaded. When the number of objects to be classified is small, it makes little sense to train an SVM to make classification decisions. But for problems that require the classification of millions of objects, supervised machine-learning techniques are currently the only feasible approach.[1]

The major disadvantages of SVMs are the converse of their strengths. First, SVMs require a great deal of time and technical expertise to im-

---

[1] Note that the scalability of SVMs relies, in part, on the fact that the difficulty of learning depends on the complexity of drawing the appropriate margin. This complexity is only indirectly related to the dimensionality of the feature space. In other words, adding features does not necessarily make drawing the boundary more difficult.

plement successfully. This project relied on internal software developed by NEC Research Laboratories; in recent years, other programs and tools supporting SVM classification have been made freely available to any interested researcher, notably Thorsten Joachims's SVM-Light and Chi-Chung Chang and Chi-Jen Lin's LIBSVM. Still, no current SVM software qualifies as easy to use, and patience and substantial programming experience are prerequisites.

Even more important, the process by which SVMs classify objects may be opaque. Decision boundaries are drawn based on many thousands of different features. SVM software does detail which features receive the most weight in drawing the decision margin. Yet these weights are difficult to interpret; moreover, the number of features that receive substantial weight may be so large that space constraints make them difficult to report. Even technical readers may balk on encountering page after page of numbers without any clear meaning.

SVMs, therefore, must ultimately be evaluated mostly by subjective criteria—by precisely the kind of complex human cognitive processes they are designed to mimic. Subjective decisions are obviously crucial in choosing the training set. The are also, ultimately, the most important metric for evaluating the accuracy of the classification decision. In the context of our research, the ideal is to have these pages coded with a consistency and accuracy identical to what human coders would provide if they were to read through these several million Web pages. The technique we relied on in this research was to sample from the machine-classified Web pages, and have the sampled sites rated blindly by human coders. The results of this comparison are explained in more detail in chapter 3, but in general it finds extremely high levels of agreement for those sites that are not close to the decision boundary. Sites about which the SVM is unsure—that is, sites that lie close to the decision margin—provided less agreement, but the large majority were coded as belonging in the positive set. This fact is likely because the training sets were filled with clear examples of relevant and irrelevant sites, and not marginal cases that may have provided more information on the proper decision boundary.

The algorithms used in SVM analysis have evolved rapidly, the software tools supporting SVM classification are improving, and the properties (and problems) of these techniques are becoming better understood. For these reasons, it is likely that coming years will see supervised learning techniques more commonly used and accepted within the social sciences.

Surfer Behavior and Crawl Depth

In addition to the use of SVM classifiers, the research in chapter 3 is also unusual in its use of large-scale Web crawlers. The principles behind these Web crawlers are easy to understand: they simply download all pages that are three clicks or less away from our seed sets. It is worth a brief detour to explain why traveling only three links away from the seed set should capture the large majority of relevant political Web sites.

The diameter of the Web is small; two randomly chosen Web sites are, on average, only nineteen hyperlinks apart (Albert, Jeong, and Barabási 1999). By traveling three links away from our seed set, our study examines graphs with a diameter of six—three links in any direction. One consequence of this property, however, is that crawling more than a few links away from the original seed set requires crawling a large fraction of the World Wide Web. In this case, increasing the depth of the crawl by one increases the number of sites that must be downloaded, stored, and analyzed by a factor of twenty.

Research on the behavior of Web surfers gives us strong reason to believe that increasing the depth of the crawl would be of limited benefit. Bernardo Huberman and his colleagues (1998) show that the number of links that a user will follow away from a starting Web site can be modeled extraordinarily well by an inverse Gaussian distribution. The probability that any path on the Web will exceed depth L is governed by the following equation:

$$P(L) = \sqrt{\frac{\gamma}{2\pi L^3}} exp\left[\frac{-\gamma(L-\mu)^2}{2\mu^2 L}\right]$$

Data taken from the unrestricted behavior of AOL users produce estimates of γ and μ of 6.24 and 2.98, respectively. While most surfing paths on the Web are only a few clicks deep, the heavy tails of the Gaussian distribution mean that even a path that contains a dozen or more clicks, contains a nontrivial portion of the probability mass.

This research suggests that the moderately deep crawl we perform should capture the large majority of surfing behavior away from the seed sites. If Huberman and his colleagues' numbers hold, roughly 80 percent of searches will terminate before exceeding the depth of the crawl we perform. And under these same assumptions, the benefits of a deeper crawl would be modest. Increasing the depth one level would expand the portion of search behavior covered by only 5 to 10 percent, while it would increase the difficulty of analysis by a factor of twenty. To provide a sense of perspective, increasing the depth of the crawl by one would have required us to download and analyze 4.5 million Web sites for *each* of the twelve crawls. This would have meant crawling roughly fifty-four million pages total, and would ultimately have taken up more than five terabytes of disk storage.

Hitwise's Data and Methodology

Lastly, much of this book is based on data from Hitwise Competitive Intelligence. In order to understand the nature of these data, it is worth outlining how and from whom they were collected, and their strengths and limitations for our purposes.

Hitwise is a multinational firm focused on measuring online traffic. Founded in Australia in 1998, Hitwise expanded its business to the United Kingdom in 2001, and the United States in 2003; Hitwise also operates in New Zealand, Hong Kong, and Singapore. Globally, Hitwise claims more than twelve hundred clients. Prominent corporate customers include Internet firms such as Google, eBay, and Ask.com, media companies such as CBS and MTV, and other a variety of other well-known brands from Honda to Heinz.

For media scholars, the Hitwise data are an enormously rich resource, offering an unparalleled view of Internet traffic at the clickstream level. Yet Hitwise data also present academic researchers with trade-offs and challenges. Some of these are already familiar to researchers who have used data prepared by corporations, such as AC Nielsen audience data or surveys prepared for consumer research (see, for example, Baum and Kernell 1999; Putnam 2000). Other issues are unique to this data source.

The Hitwise data are gathered in partnership with Internet service providers; Hitwise creates software that its partners then install within their networks. Hitwise's software monitors the online traffic of the Internet service providers' subscribers; for the month of April 2007, Hitwise tracked visits to 773,924 Web sites from ten million U.S. households. The number of sites included in the Hitwise panel fluctuates constantly. This fluctuation comes from three main sources. First, Hitwise includes sites in its ranking if they exceed some minimum of Web traffic. It is for this reason that Hitwise's monthly data include a greater number of Web sites than Hitwise's weekly data; the longer time span allows more sites to reach the traffic threshold required for inclusion. Second, Hitwise regularly audits the sites included in its rankings, removing outdated entries. Third, Hitwise's portfolio of Internet service provider partners does shift somewhat over time, with new partners added and some old ones removed.

Twenty-five percent of the ten million users in the Hitwise sample also participate in opt-in "megapanels," run by companies such as Experian and Claritas. These opt-in panelists provide much more detailed demographic, lifestyle, consumer data. Ultimately, the Internet service providers supply Hitwise only with anonymized, aggregate data. Hitwise does not release the names of its partners. Nevertheless, Hitwise (2007) does state that its sample "include[s] some of the top ISPs as well as a geographically diverse range of middle tier and small ISPs, representing both home and work usage."

Hitwise uses this sample to construct a variety of industry standard usage metrics. Many of these traffic measures are defined by the Interactive Advertising Bureau, a nonprofit advertising-industry consortium. (The bureau claims that its member companies are responsible for selling more than 86 percent of online advertising in the United States.) The most important measure for our purpose is the number of "visits" a site receives. A visit is described as a request for a Web page by a browser, with no more than thirty minutes between clicks. Note that this metric records use that is frequent, but not too frequent; a single individual who spent all day reading CNN.com would count as one visit.

Hitwise does measure the number of page views that individual sites serve to users, but this metric is problematic. One reason for this is that page counts are highly dependent on the architecture of a Web site. Some online publications, for example, deliberately break up their content to force users to load many short pages; others do not. Because this metric is not comparable across Web sites, it is not referred to in the text. It is worth noting, however, that page counts produce far higher levels of inequality than site visits. MySpace alone accounted for 18 percent of all page views on the Web during April 2007. For political sites, too, an analysis of page views would suggest far higher levels of inequality than that seen with site visits alone.

Hitwise's method of monitoring has clear strengths and weaknesses. One key strength is scalability. Incredibly, the Hitwise sample represents nearly one in ten households nationwide, according to the U.S. Census Bureau (2001). For smaller online niches, such breadth of coverage is indispensable.

Hitwise's methodology is also far better than the alternatives in gathering a representative cross-section of Web traffic. Traffic is measured across all users, not just those willing to install monitoring software on their computer. Because most of Hitwise's sample is unaware that their search behavior is being measured, any observer effect should be minimal.

For individual-level analysis, Hitwise data are (by design) quite limited. Hitwise's methods allow us to see the sum of users' online paths, but picking particular surfers out of this flow of traffic is not possible. Not only does Hitwise average user behavior, it allows researchers to look only at sites visited immediately before and after the site or category of interest.

Deeper patterns in user online behavior are thus obscured. For example, we might imagine that surfers who enter a political blog from a search engine may exhibit different characteristics and search behaviors than those referred by another blog. If this is true, it cannot be studied with the Hitwise data.

Still, given privacy concerns, some of these limits are reassuring. For instance, in August 2006, AOL released search records that included twenty million search requests from more than 657,000 of its subscribers. (Pass, Chowdhury, and Torgeson 2006). Though AOL's data were intended to be anonymous, the data set listed users by a unique user identification number; the search queries themselves sometimes contained individually identifying information, particularly in combination with one another.

The fact that some details of Hitwise's methodology and corporate agreements remain proprietary or confidential may raise flags, especially for academic users. Several factors partly assuage these concerns. First, Hitwise has arranged for detailed, independent audits of its methodology and data collection procedures. Recent audits have been performed by PriceWaterhouseCoopers, which concluded that the company's claims about its data-gathering methodology, and its claims about the representativeness of its sample, were truthful and accurate. (PriceWaterhouse-Coopers also certified that Hitwise's privacy policies did indeed operate as claimed.)

Second, many of Hitwise's clients are large Internet companies such as Google and eBay. These firms have extensive in-house expertise in analyzing Web traffic as well as access to large data sets of their own with which to cross-validate Hitwise's measures. It would be difficult to hide significant methodological flaws from such clients.

Third, in April 2007 Hitwise agreed to be acquired by the Experian Group, a credit- and consumer-information firm based in Ireland, for the sum of $240 million. Experian is a publicly traded company, and Hitwise's claims about its methodology were reiterated in corporate legal disclosures related to the purchase. Any misleading claims in this context, of course, can subject corporate officers to civil and criminal penalties.

For those interested in large-scale Internet traffic analysis— particularly in a niche as small as political Web sites—there are few alternatives to Hitwise. Hitwise's main competitors are Nielsen//NetRatings and comScore MediaMetrix. Each of these companies rely almost entirely on an opt-in panel methodology, recruiting users to install Internet-monitoring software on their computers. Users are offered incentives to participate; for example, comScore offers participants server-based virus scanning and sweepstakes prizes. Panelists know that their Internet usage is being individually monitored, which may alter their online behavior. ComScore claims to have a nationwide sample of 120,000 users, or slightly more than 1 percent of Hitwise's U.S. sample.

Nielsen//NetRatings and comScore have resisted independent audits of their panel methodologies in the past, despite reports of problems and inconsistencies with their data. These concerns came to a head in April 2007, when the Interactive Advertising Bureau strongly criticized their panel methodology and demanded that both firms submit to independent audits (Rothenberg 2007). The bureau's demands prompted both companies to promise greater accountability and transparency in their methods. Thus far, it remains unclear what changes will be made.

References

Abbatte, J. 1998. *Inventing the Internet.* Cambridge, MA: MIT Press.

Abramowitz, A. I., J. McGlennon, R. B. Rapoport, and W. J. Stone. 2001. "Activists in the United States Presidential Nomination Process, 1980–1996." Computer file. 2nd ICPSR version. Study no. 6143. http://webapp.icpsr.umich.edu/cocoon/ICPSR-STUDY/06143.xml.

Ackerman, B. A., and J. S. Fishkin. 2004. *Deliberation Day.* New Haven, CT: Yale University Press.

Adamic, L. A., and N. Glance. 2005. "The Political Blogosphere and the 2004 U.S. Election: Divided They Blog." In *LinkKDD '05: Proceedings of the 3rd International Workshop on Link Discovery*, 36–43. http://dx.doi.org/10.1145/1134271.1134277. New York: ACM Press.

Adamic, L. A., and B. A. Huberman. 2000. "The Nature of Markets on the World Wide Web." *Quarterly Journal of Economic Commerce* 1:5–12.

Albert, A., H. Jeong, and A. -L. Barabási. 1999. "Diameter of the World Wide Web." *Nature* 401:130–31.

Allen, M. 2007. "Move Over, MoveOn: GOP's A-Comin'." *Politico*, June 29. http://www.politico.com/news/stories/0607/4712.html.

Althaus, S. 2007. "Free Falls, High Dives, and the Future of Democratic Accountability." Paper presented at the Changing Media and Political Accountability conference, Center for the Study of Democratic Politics, Princeton University, November 30–December 1.

Amazon.com, Inc. 2005. *Annual Report.* http://edgar.sec.gov.

American Society of Newspaper Editors. 1997. *The Journalists.* Report, July Reston, VA. http://www.asne.org/kiosk/reports/97reports/journalists90s/journalists.html.

Anderson, C. 2004. "The Long Tail." *Wired.* http://www.wired.com/wired/archive/12.10/tail.htm.

———. 2006a. *The Long Tail.* New York: Hyperion.

———. 2006b. "We Did It!" Blog post July 11. http://www.thelongtail.com/the_long_tail/2006/07/we_did_it.html.

Armstrong, J., and M. Moulitsas Zuniga. 2006. *Crashing the Gates: Netroots, Grassroots, and the Rise of People-Powered Politics.* White River Junction, VT: Chelsea Green.

Arnold, R. D. 1990. *The Logic of Congressional Action.* New Haven, CT: Yale University Press.

Ashbee, E. 2003. "The Lott Resignation, 'Blogging,' and American Conservatism." *Political Quarterly* 74:361–70.

Ayres, C. 2005. "Million Lawyers a Legal Nightmare." *Times* (London), February 26. http://www.timesonline.co.uk/article/0,,11069-1500707,00.html.

Baker, S., H. Green, and R. D. Hof. 2004. "Click the Vote." *Businessweek,* March 29, 102.

Barabási, A. -L. 2002. *Linked.* Cambridge, MA: Perseus Publishing.

Barabási, A. -L., and R. Albert. 1999. "Emergence of Scaling in Random Networks." *Science* 286:509–12.

Barabási, A. -L., R. Albert, H. Jeong, and G. Bianconi. 2000. "Power-Law Distribution of the World Wide Web." *Science* 287:12–13.

Barnes and Noble, Inc. 2005. *Annual Report.* http://edgar.sec.gov.

Barnouw, E. 1966. *A Tower in Babel.* Oxford: Oxford University Press.

Bartels, L. M. 1988. *Presidential Primaries and the Dynamics of Public Choice.* Princeton, NJ: Princeton University Press.

Bartlett, B. 2003. "Blog On." *National Review Online,* January 6. http://www.nationalreview.com/nrofbartlett/bartlett010603.asp.

Baum, M. A., and S. Kernell. 1999. "Has Cable Ended the Golden Age of Presidential Television?" *American Political Science Review* 93:99–114.

Bear, N. Z. 2004. "Weblogs by Average Daily Traffic." http://www.truthlaidbear.com/TrafficRanking.php (accessed December 5, 2004).

Benkler, Y. 2006. *The Wealth of Networks: How Social Production Transforms Markets and Freedom.* New Haven, CT: Yale University Press.

Bennett, W. L. 2003a. "The Burglar Alarm That Just Keeps Ringing: A Response to Zaller." *Political Communication* 20:131–38.

———. 2003b. "Communicating Global Activism: Strengths and Vulnerabilities of Networked Politics." *Information, Communications, and Society* 6:143–68.

Berkowitz, P. 1996. "The Debating Society." *New Republic*, November 25, 36–42.

Berman, A. 2008. "The Dean Legacy." *Nation*, March 17. http://www.thenation.com/doc/20080317/berman.

Berners-Lee, T. 2000. *Weaving the Web*. New York: HarperBusiness.

Bimber, B. 1998. "The Internet and Political Transformation: Populism, Community, and Accelerated Pluralism." *Polity* 31:133–60.

———. 2000. "The Gender Gap on the Internet." *Social Science Quarterly* 81: 868–76.

———. 2001. "Information and Political Engagement in America: The Search for Effects of Information Technology at the Individual Level." *Political Research Quarterly* 54:53–67.

———. 2003a. *Information and American Democracy: Technology in the Evolution of Political Power*. Cambridge: Cambridge University Press.

———. 2003b. "Notes on the Diffusion of the Internet." Report. University of California at Santa Barbara. http://www.polsci.ucsb.edu/faculty/bimber/Internet-Diffusion.htm.

Bimber, B., and R. Davis. 2003. *Campaigning Online: The Internet in U.S. Elections*. New York: Oxford University Press.

Bishop, T. 2004. "Bloggers Rule the Day in Earliest Reporting." *Baltimore Sun*, November 3, 13B.

"Blog-Hopping." 2004. *Columbus Dispatch*, July 12, 06A.

Bloom, J. D. 2003. "The Blogosphere: How a Once Humble Medium Came to Drive Elite Discourse and Influence Public Policy and Elections." Paper presented at the 2003 annual meeting of the American Political Science Association, Philadelphia, August 28.

Boczkowski, P. J. 2005. *Digitizing the News: Innovation in Online Newspapers*. Cambridge, MA: MIT Press.

Borenstein, S., and G. Saloner. 2001. "Economics and Electronic Commerce." *Journal of Economic Perspectives* 15:3–12.

Boyle, J. 1996. *Shamans, Software, and Spleens: Law and the Construction of the Information Society*. Cambridge, MA: Harvard University Press.

Brin, S., and L. Page. 1998. "The Anatomy of a Large-Scale Hypertextual Web Search Engine." *Computer Networks and ISDN Systems* 30: 107–17.

Bromage, A. W. 1930. "Literacy and the Electorate." *American Political Science Review* 24:946–62.

Brown, M. 1994. "Using Gini-Style Indices to Evaluate the Spatial Patterns of Health Practitioners: Theoretical Considerations and an Application Based on Alberta Data." *Social Science Medicine* 38:1243–56.

Brynjolfsson, E., and L. M. Hitt. 2000. "Beyond Computation: Information Technology, Organizational Transformation, and Business Performance." *Journal of Economic Perspectives* 14:23–48.

Campbell, K. 2002. "You, Too, Can Have a Voice in Blogland." *Christian Science Monitor*, June 19, Features sec. p. 12.

Cappelli, P., and M. Hamori. 2004. "The Path to the Top." National Bureau of Economic Research working paper no. w10507. http://www.nber.org/papers/w10507.

Castells, M. 2000. *The Information Age: Economy, Society, Culture.* Oxford: Blackwell.

Cederman, L. -E. 2003. "Modeling the Size of Wars: From Billiard Balls to Sand Piles." *American Political Science Review* 97:135–50.

Center for Responsive Politics (CRP) 2004. *Report on 2004 Donor Demographics.* http://www.opensecrets.org/presidential/donordems.asp.

Chaddock, G. R. 2005. "Their Clout Rising, Blogs Are Courted by Washington's Elite." *Christian Science Monitor*, October 27, USA Sec., 1.

Chadwick, A. 2006 *Internet Politics.* Oxford: Oxford University Press.

Cho, J., and S. Roy. 2004. "Impact of Search Engines on Page Popularity." In *WWW '04: Proceedings of the 13th International Conference on the World Wide Web*, 20–29. New York: ACM Press.

Cleaver, H. M., Jr. 1998. "The Zapatista Effect: The Internet and the Rise of an Alternative Political Fabric." *Journal of International Affairs* 51:621–22.

Cohen, A. 2006. "Why the Democratic Ethic of the World Wide Web May Be about to End." *New York Times.* Editorial observer, May 28. http://www.nytimes.com/2006/05/28/opinion/28sun3.html.

Cohen, J. 1989. "Deliberation and Democratic Legitimacy." In *The Good Polity*, ed. A. Hamlin and P. Pettit, 17–34. Oxford: Blackwell.

Colford, P. D. 2004. "Big Blog Bucks." *New York Daily News*, October 5, 52.

Connolly-Ahern, C., A. P. Williams, and L. L. Kaid. 2003. "Hyperlinking as Gatekeeping: Online Newspaper Coverage of the Execution of an American Terrorist." *Journalism Studies* 4:401–14.

Cornfield, M., and L. Raine. 2003. *Untuned Keyboards: Online Campaigners, Citizens, and Portals in the 2002 Elections.* Washington, DC: Institute for Politics, Democracy, and the Internet.

Cortes, C., and V. Vapnik. 1995. "Support-Vector Networks." *Machine Learning* 20:273–97.

Crowe, R. 2005. "Bush, Kerry Aides Reflect on '04 Campaign." *Houston Chronicle*, January 27, A11.

U.S. Census Bureau. 2001. "Households and Families." Census 2000 brief, Washington, DC, September. http://www.census.gov/prod/2001pubs/c2kbr01-8.pdf.

Curtin, M. 2000. "Gatekeeping in the Neo-Network Era." In *Advocacy Groups and the Entertainment Industry*, ed. M. Suman and G. Rossman. Westport, CT: Praeger, 217–46.

Davis, R. 1998. *The Web of Politics.* Oxford: Oxford University Press.

Deibert, R. J. 2000. "International Plug 'n' Play? Citizen Activism, the Internet, and Global Public Policy." *International Studies Perspectives* 1:255–72.

———. 2003. "Black Code: Censorship, Surveillance, and the Militarization of Cyberspace." Paper presented at the International Studies Association Conference, Portland, OR, February 25.

Dertouzos, J. N., and W. B. Trautman. 1990. "Economic Effects of Media Concentration: Estimates from a Model of the Newspaper Firm." *Journal of Industrial Economics* 39:1–14.

Dijk, J.A.G.M.V. 2005. *The Deepening Divide: Inequality in the Information Society.* Thousand Oaks, CA: Sage Publications.

Dill, S., R. Kumar, K. S. McCurley, S. Rajagopalan, D. Sivakumar, and A. Tomkins. 2002. "Self-Similarity in the Web." *ACM Transactions on Internet Technology* 2:205–23.

DiMaggio, P., E. Hargittai, C. Ceste, and S. Shafer. 2004. "Digital Inequality: From Unequal Access to Differentiated Use." In *Social Inequality*, ed. K. Neckerman, 355–400. New York: Russell Sage Foundation.

Ding, C., X. He, P. Husbands, H. Zha, and H. Simon. 2002. "PageRank, HITS, and a Unified Framework for Link Analysis." Berkeley, CA: Lawrence Berkeley National Laboratory.

Drezner, D. W., and H. Farrell. 2004a. "The Power and Politics of Blogs." Paper presented at the annual meeting of the American Political Science Association, Chicago, September 2–5.

———. 2004b. "Web of Influence." *Foreign Policy* 145:32–40.

Drum, K. 2005. "Of Blogs and Men." Blog entry February 18. http://www.washingtonmonthly.com/archives/individual/005685.php.

Dryzek, J. S. 2002. *Deliberative Democracy and Beyond: Liberals, Critics, Contestations.* Oxford: Oxford University Press.

Epstein, E. J. 1974. *News from Nowhere: Television and the News.* New York: Vintage Books.

Falcone, M. 2003. "Dear Campaign Diary: Seizing the Day, Online." *New York Times*, September 11, G1.

Faler, B. 2004a. "Online, Political, and Influential; Survey: Visitors to Candidate Web Sites Are Opinion Leaders." *Washington Post*, February 9, A05.

———. 2004b. "Some Candidates Turn to Blogs to Place Ads; Sites Are Low-Cost, Reach Thousands." *Washington Post*, April 18, A05.

Fallows, D. 2005. *Search Engine Users*. January 23. Washington, DC: Pew Internet and American Life Project.

Faloutsos, M., P. Faloutsos, and C. Faloutsos. 1999. "On Power-Law Relationships of the Internet Topology." In *SIGCOMM*, 251–62.

Fasoldt, A. 2003. "The Mighty Blog: Lott Saga a Milestone for Online Pundits." *New Orleans Times-Picayune*, January 8, Living sec., 3.

Fishman, M. 1980. *Manufacturing the News*. Austin: University of Texas Press.

Foot, K., and S. Schneider. 2006. *Web Campaigning*. Cambridge, MA: MIT Press.

Fortunato, S., A. Flammini, F. Menczer, and A. Vespignani. 2006. "The Egalitarian Effect of Search Engines." *Proceedings of the National Academy of Sciences* 103:12684–89.

Franklin, C. H. 1992. "Measurement and the Dynamics of Party Identification." *Political Behavior* 14:297–309.

Frantzich, S. 2004. "Technology and the U.S. Congress: Looking Back and Looking Forward." *Information Polity* 9:103–13.

Gamson, J. 2003. "Gay Media, Inc.: Media Structures, the New Gay Conglomerates, and Collective Sexual Identities." In *Cyberactivism: Online Activism in Theory and Practice*, ed. M. McCaughey and M. D. Ayers, 255–79. London: Routledge.

Gandy, O. H. 2002. "The Real Digital Divide: Citizens versus Consumers." In *The Handbook of New Media*, ed. L. Lievrouw and S. Livingstone, 448–60. Thousand Oaks, CA: Sage Publications.

Gans, H. J. 1980. *Deciding What's News*. New York: Vintage Books.

Garrido, M., and A. Halavais. 2003. "Mapping Networks of Support for the Zapatista Movement." In *Cyberactivism: Online Activism in Theory and Practice*, ed. M. McCaughey and M. D. Ayers, 165–84. London: Routledge.

Gates, B. 2000. *Business at the Speed of Thought: Succeed in the Digital Economy*. New York: Warner Business Books.

Geras, N. 2004. "The Normblog Profile 16: Glenn Reynolds." Interview, January 9. http://normblog.typepad.com/normblog/2004/01/the_normblog_pr_1.html.

Gillmor, D. 2004. *We the Media*. Cambridge, MA: O'Reilly.

Gini, C. 1921. "Measurement of Inequality of Incomes." *Economic Journal* 31:124–26.

Google, Inc. 2005. *Annual Report*. http://edgar.sec.gov.

Green, D. P., B. Palmquist, and E. Schickler. 2002. *Partisan Hearts and Minds: Political Parties and the Social Identities of Voters*. New Haven, CT: Yale University Press.

Grossman, L. K. 1995. *The Electronic Republic: Reshaping Democracy in the Information Age*. New York: Viking Penguin.

Guthrie, J. 2004. "Fellow Anchors Defend Rather on Forged Papers." *San Francisco Chronicle*, October 3, A2.

Gutmann, A., and D. Thompson. 1996. *Democracy and Disagreement*. Cambridge, MA: Harvard University Press.

Habermas, J. 1981. *The Theory of Communicative Action*. London: Beacon Press.

———. 1996. *Between Facts and Norms: Contributions to a Discourse Theory of Law and Democracy*. Cambridge, MA: MIT Press.

Hafner, K. 1998. *Where Wizards Stay Up Late*. New York: Simon and Schuster.

Halloran, L. 2004. "Slogging through Convention Blogs." *Hartford Courant*, July 29, D1.

Hamilton, J. T. 2004. *All the News That's Fit to Sell: How the Market Transforms Information into News*. Princeton, NJ: Princeton University Press.

Hansell, S. 2006. "Google Posts 60% Gain in Earnings." *New York Times*. http://www.nytimes.com/2006/04/21/technology/21google.htm.

Hargittai, E. 2000. "Open Portals or Closed Gates? Channeling Content on the World Wide Web." *Poetics* 27:233–53.

———. 2003. "How Wide a Web? Inequalities in Accessing Information Online." PhD diss., Princeton University.

Hartlaub, P. 2004a. "Unbound by Tradition, Boston Bloggers Exercise Fresh Freedom of the Press." *San Francisco Chronicle*, July 30, E1.

———. 2004b. "Web Sites Provide Alternative to Wary TV Coverage." *San Francisco Chronicle*, November 3, A14.

Healy, P., and J. Zeleny. 2008. "Obama Outshines Clinton at Raising Funds." *New York Times*, February 8. http://www.nytimes.com/2008/02/08/us/politics/08clinton.html.

Herring, S. 2002. "Searching for Safety Online: Managing 'Trolling' in a Feminist Forum." *Information Society* 18:371–84.

Hewitt, H. 2005. *Blog: Understanding the Information Reformation That's Changing Your World*. Nashville, TN: Nelson Books.

Hirschman, A. O. 1964. "The Paternity of an Index." *American Economic Review* 54:761–62.

Hitwise. 2007. "Methodology FAQ." Hitwise Competitive Intelligence. http://clients.hitwise.com/faq/index.html.

Horn, J. 2004. "Exit Polls Bog Down the Blogs." *Los Angeles Times*, November 3, A33.

Howard, P. N. 2005. *New Media Campaigns and the Managed Citizen*. New York: Cambridge University Press.

Huberman, B. A. 2001. *Laws of the Web*. Cambridge, MA: MIT Press.

Huberman, B. A., P.L.T. Pirolli, J. E. Pitkow, and R. M. Lukose. 1998. "Strong Regularities in World Wide Web Surfing." *Science* 280:95–97.

Introna, L. D., and H. Nissenbaum. 2000. "Shaping the Web: Why the Politics of Search Engines Matters." *Information Society* 16:169–85.

Jansen, B. J., and A. Spink. 2006. "How Are We Searching the World Wide Web? A Comparison of Nine Search Engine Transaction Logs." *Information Processing and Management* 42:248–63.

Jansen, B. J., A. Spink, J. Bateman, and T. Saracevic. 1998. "Real Life Information Retrieval: A Study of User Queries on the Web." *SIGIR Forum* 32:5–17.

Jennings, M. K., and V. Zeitner. 2003. "Internet Use and Civic Engagement: A Longitudinal Analysis." *Public Opinion Quarterly* 67:311–34.

Joachims, T. 1998. "Text Categorization with Support Vector Machines: Learning with Many Relevant Features." In *Proceedings of ECML-98, 10th European Conference on Machine Learning*, ed. C. Nédellec and C. Rouveirol, 137–42. Heidelberg: Springer Verlag.

Johnson, D. B., and J. R. Gibson. 1974. "The Divisive Primary Revisited: Party Activists in Iowa." *American Political Science Review* 68:67–77.

Johnson, T. J., and B. K. Kaye. 2003. "A Boost or Bust for Democracy?" *Harvard International Journal of Press and Politics* 8:9–34.

———. 2004. "Wag the Blog: How Reliance on Traditional Media and the Internet Influence Credibility Perceptions of Weblogs among Blog Users." *Journalism and Mass Communication Quarterly* 81:622–42.

Justice, G. 2004. "Kerry Kept Money Coming with Internet as His ATM." *New York Times*, November 6, A12.

Kahn, R., and D. Kellner. 2004. "New Media and Internet Activism: From the Battle of Seattle to Blogging." *New Media and Society* 6:87–95.

Karmark, E. C., and J. S. Nye, eds. 2002. *Governance.com: Democracy in the Information Age*. Washington, DC: Brookings.

Kayany, J. M. 1998. "Contexts of Uninhibited Online Behavior: Flaming in Social Newsgroups on Usenet." *Journal of the American Society for Information Science* 49:1135–41.

Kelley, S. 1962. "Campaign Debate: Some Facts and Figures." *Public Opinion Quarterly* 26:351–66.

Kessler, J. 2004. "Call of the Blog." *Atlanta Journal-Constitution*. August 17, 1JJ.

Kleinberg. J. M. 1999. "Authoritative Sources in a Hyperlinked Environment." *Journal of the ACM* 46:604–32.

Klotz, R. J. 2004. *The Politics of Internet Communication*. New York: Rowman and Littlefield.

Knight Ridder, Inc. 2005. *Annual Report.* http://edgar.sec.gov.

Kohut, A. 2005. "The Dean Activists: Their Profile and Prospects." April 6. Washington, DC: Pew Research Center for People and the Press.

Kornblum, J. 2003. "Welcome to the Blogosphere." *USA Today*, July 8, 7D.

Krueger, B. S. 2002. "Assessing the Impact of Internet Political Participation in the United States: A Resource Approach." *American Political Research* 30:476–98.

Krugman, P. 1994. "Complex Landscapes in Economic Geography." *American Economic Review* 84:412–16.

Kumar, R., P. Raghavan, S. Rajagopalan, and A. Tomkins. 1999. "Trawling the Web for Emerging Cyber-communities." *Computer Networks* 31:1481–93.

Last, J. V. 2002. "Reading, Writing, and Blogging." *Weekly Standard*, March 14. http://www.weeklystandard.com/Content/Public/Articles/000/000/001/009flofq.asp.

Lawrence, S., and C. L. Giles. 1998. "Searching the World Wide Web." *Science* 280:98–100.

Lebert, J. 2003. "Wiring Human Rights Activism: Amnesty International and the Challenges of Information and Communication Technologies." In *Cyberactivism: Online Activism in Theory and Practice*, ed. M. McCaughey and M. Ayers, 209–32. London: Routledge.

LeCun, Y., L. Jackel, L. Bottou, A. Brunot, C. Cortes, J. Denker, H. Drucker, I. Guyon, U. Muller, E. Sackinger, P. Simard, and V. Vapnik. 1995. "Comparison of Learning Algorithms for Handwritten Digit Recognition." In *International Conference on Artificial Neural Networks*, ed. F. Fogelmon and P. Gallinari, 53–60. Paris: EC2 et Cie.

Lenhart, A., and S. Fox. 2006. *Bloggers: A Picture of the Internet's New Storytellers*. Washington, DC: Pew Internet and American Life Project. http://www.pewinternet.org/PPF/r/186/report_display.asp.

Lenhart, A., J. Horrrigan, L. Rainie, A. Boyce, M. Madden, and E. O'Grady. 2003. "The Ever-Shifting Internet Population: A New Look at Internet Access and the Digital Divide." April 16. Washington, DC: Pew Internet and American Life Project.

Lentz, J. 2001. *Electing Jesse Ventura*. Boulder, CO: Lynne Rienner Publishers.

Lessig, L. 1999. *Code and Other Laws of Cyberspace*. New York: Basic Books.

———. 2001. *The Future of Ideas*. New York: Random House.

Levey, N. M. 2006. "Anti-Foley Blogger Speaks Out." *Los Angeles Times*, November 10, A13.

Lewin, K. 1947. "Frontiers in Group Dynamics." *Human Relations* 1 (2): 143–53.

Lijphart, A. 1997. "Unequal Participation: Democracy's Unresolved Dilemma." *American Political Science Review* 91:1–14.

Liljeros, F., C. R. Edling, L. A. Nunes Amaral, H. E. Stanley, and Y. Aberg. 2001. "The Web of Human Sexual Contacts." *Nature* 411:907–8.

Lillkvist, M. 2004. "Advertising Sales Take Off on Internet Blogs." *Wall Street Journal*, March 16, D6.

Littan, R. E., and A. M. Rivlin. 2001. "Projecting the Economic Impact of the Internet." *American Economic Review* 91:313–17.

Lohr, S., and S. Hansell. 2006. "Microsoft and Google Set to Wage Arms Race." *New York Times*. http://www.nytimes.com/2006/05/02/technology/02google.html.

Lucking-Reiley, D., and D. F. Spulber. 2001. "Business-to-Business Electronic Commerce." *Journal of Economic Perspectives* 15:55–68.

Luo, M. 2008. "Small Online Contributions Add Up to a Huge Edge for Obama." *New York Times*, February 20. http://www.nytimes.com/2008/02/20/us/politics/20obama.html.

Lupia, A., and G. Sin. 2003. "Which Public Goods Are Endangered? How Evolving Communications Technologies Affect *The Logic of Collective Action.*" *Public Choice* 117:315–31.

Macedo, S., Y. Alex-Assensoh, J. M. Berry, M. Brintnall, D. E. Campbell, L. R. Fraga, A. Fung, W. A. Galston, C. F. Karpowitz, M. Levi, M. Levinson, K. Lipsitz, R. G. Niemi, R. D. Putnam, W. M. Rahn, R. Reich, R. R. Rodgers, T. Swanstrom, and K. C. Walsh. 2005. *Democracy at Risk: How Political Choices Undermine Citizen Participation and What We Can Do about It.* Washington, DC: Brookings Institution Press.

MacIntyre, B. 2004. "Welcome to the New Tom Paines." *London Times*, November 13, 30.

Malcolm, A. 2008. "News Shocker: Ron Paul Was Biggest GOP Fundraiser Last Quarter." *Los Angeles Times*, Top of the Ticket blog, February 2. http://latimesblogs.latimes.com/washington/2008/02/news-shocker-ro.html.

Manuel, M. 2004. "Boston E-Party." *Atlanta Journal-Constitution*, July 25, 1E.

Marendy, P. 2001. "A Review of World Wide Web Searching Techniques, Focusing on HITS and Related Algorithms That Utilise the Link Topology of the World Wide Web to Provide the Basis for a Structure-Based Search Technology." Working paper, James Cook University, North Queensland, Australia.

Margolis, M., and D. Resnick. 2000. *Politics as Usual: The Cyberspace "Revolution."* Thousand Oaks, CA: Sage Publications.

Martinez, J. 2004. "Wild, Wild Web." *Denver Post*, August 13, B07.

Matheson, D. 2004. "Weblogs and the Epistemology of the News: Some Trends in Online Journalism." *New Media and Society* 6:443–68.

May, C. 2002. *The Information Society: A Sceptical View*. Cambridge, UK: Polity Press.

McCarthy, E. 2004. "Beltway Bloggers; Personal Politics Turn Communal on a Web of Local Internet Sites." *Washington Post*, February 7, E01.

McChesney, R. W. 1990. "The Battle for the U.S. Airwaves, 1928–1935." *Journal of Communication* 40:29–57.

McCubbins, M. D., and T. Schwartz. 1984. "Congressional Oversight Overlooked: Police Patrols versus Fire Alarms." *American Journal of Political Science* 28:165–79.

McLaine, S. 2003. "Ethnic Online Communities: Between Profit and Purpose." In *Cyberactivism: Online Activism in Theory and Practice*, ed. M. McCaughey and M. D. Ayers, 233–54. London: Routledge.

Megna, M. 2002. "Web Logs Enable Anyone with an Opinion to Be Heard." *New York Daily News*, November 10, Lifeline sec., 6.

Memmott, M. 2004. "Blogs, Journalism: Different Factions of the Write Wing." *USA Today*, July 27, 6A.

Meyer, P. 1995. "Learning to Love Lower Profits." *American Journalism Review*, December, 40–44.

Miller, W. E., and J. M. Shanks. 1996. *The New American Voter*. Cambridge, MA: Harvard University Press.

Morahan–Martin, J. M. 2004. "How Internet Users Find, Evaluate, and Use Online Health Information: A Cross-cultural Review." *Cyberpsychology and Behavior* 7:497–510.

Morse, R. 2004. "Web Forum Shapes Political Thinking: Dem Consultant in Berkeley Builds Blog into Influential Tool." *San Francisco Chronicle*, January 15. http://sfgate.com/cgi-bin/article.cgi?f=/c/a/2004 /01/15/ BAGR14A8Q71.DTL.

Mossberger, K., C. J. Tolbert, and M. Stansbury. 2003. *Virtual Inequality: Beyond the Digital Divide*. Washington, DC: Georgetown University Press.

Nagourney, A. 2003. "For Democrats, an Early Chance to Sample the 2004 Line of Presidential Candidates." *New York Times*, February 22, A11.

National Advisory Council on Radio in Education (NACRE). 1937. *Four Years of Network Broadcasting*. Chicago: University of Chicago Press. Report of the National Committee on Radio in Education and the American Political Science Association.

National Telecommunications and Information Administration (NTIA). 2000. *Falling through the Net: Toward Digital Inclusion*. Report, February. Washington, DC: National Telecommunications and Information Administration.

———. 2002. *A Nation Online: How Americans Are Expanding Their Use of the Internet*. Report, February. Washington, DC: National Telecommunications and Information Administration.

Negroponte, N. 1995. *Being Digital*. New York: Knopf.

Nevius, C. W. 2004. "Blogs Alter Political Landscape." *San Francisco Chronicle*, November 2, B1.

New York Times Digital. 2004. "Site Statistics." http://www.nytdigital.com /learn/statistics.html (accessed January 2005).

New York Times, Inc. 2005. *Annual Report.* http://edgar.sec.gov.

Nielsen, J. 1999. *Designing Web Usability: The Practice of Simplicity.* New York: New Riders Press.

Nino, C. S. 1998. *The Constitution of Deliberative Democracy.* New Haven, CT: Yale University Press.

Noam, E. 2003. "The Internet: Still Wide Open and Competitive?" OII issue brief no. 1. Oxford: Oxford Internet Institute.

———. 2004. "How to Measure Media Concentration." *Financial Times,* September 7, 15.

Norris, P. 2001. *Digital Divide: Civic Engagement, Information Poverty, and the Internet in Democratic Societies.* New York: Cambridge University Press.

O'Gorman, K. 2007. "Brian Williams Weighs in on New Medium." *We Want Media,* April 6. http://journalism.nyu.edu/pubzone/wewantmedia/ node/487.

Orwell, G. 1946. "Politics and the English Language." *Horizon* (London). April.

Osuna, E., R. Freund, and F. Girosi. 1997. "An Improved Training Algorithm for Support Vector Machines." In *Neural Networks for Signal Processing: Proceedings of the TEEE Workshop,* Amelia Island, FL, September 24–26, 276–85.

Owen, B. M. 1999. *The Internet Challenge to Television.* Cambridge, MA: Harvard University Press.

Page, B. I., and R. Y. Shapiro. 1992. *The Rational Public: Fifty Years of Trends in Americans' Policy Preferences.* Chicago: University of Chicago Press.

Pandurangan, G., P. Raghavan, and E. Upfal. 2002. "Using PageRank to Characterize Web Structure." Paper presented at the annual International Computing and Combinatorics conference, *(COCOON),* Singapore, August 15–17.

Pareto, V. 1897. *Cours d'Economie Politique.* Vol. 2. Lausanne: F. Rouge.

Pass, G., A. Chowdhury, and C. Torgeson. 2006. "A Picture of Search." In *Proceedings of the 1st International Conference on Scalable Information Systems.* New York: ACM Press.

Pennock, D. M., G. W. Flake, S. Lawrence, E. J. Glover, and C. L. Giles. 2002. "Winners Don't Take All: Characterizing the Competition for Links on the Web." *Proceedings of the National Academy of Sciences* 99:5207–11.

Perrone, J. 2004. "Online: Blog Watch: Unconventional." *Guardian,* July 29, 20.

Pew Center for People and the Press. 2006. "Online Papers Modestly Boost Newspaper Readership." Washington, DC, July 30. http://pewresearch .org/pubs/238/online-papers-modestly-boost-newspaper-readership.

Picard, R. G. 2002. *The Economics and Financing of Media Companies*. New York: Fordham University Press.

Platt J. 1998. Sequential Minimal Optimization: A Fast Algorithm for Training Support Vector Machines. Technical report no. 98–14. Microsoft Research, Redmond, Washington, April. http://www.research.microsoft.com/jplatt/smo.html.

Postmes, T., and S. Brunsting. 2002. "Collective Action in the Age of the Internet." *Social Science Computer Review* 20:290–301.

Powell, M. K. 2002. Remarks of the FCC Chairman at the Broadband Technology Summit, U.S. Chamber of Commerce, Washington, DC, April 30. http://www.fcc.gov/Speeches/Powell/2002/spmkp205.html.

Prior, M. 2007. *Post-Broadcast Democracy*. New York: Cambridge University Press.

Project for Excellence in Journalism. 2007. *State of the News Media 2007*. Washington, DC. http://www.stateofthenewsmedia.com/2007/.

Putnam, R. D. 2000. *Bowling Alone: The Collapse and Revival of American Community*. New York: Simon and Schuster.

Quindlen, A. 2006. "The Glass Half Empty." *New York Times*, November 22, A27.

Ranie, L. 2005. "The State of Blogging." Data memo, January. Washington, DC: Pew Internet and American Life Project. http://www.pewinterne-www.pewinternet.org/pdfs/PIP_blogging_data.pdf.

Rapoport, R. B., and W. J. Stone, 1999. "National Survey of Callers to the Perot 1-800 Numbers, 1992." Computer file. ICPSR version. Study no. 2809. http://webapp.icpsr.umich.edu/cocoon/ICPSR-STUDY/06143.xml.

Rawls, J. 1995 *Political Liberalism*. New York: Columbia University Press.

Reddaway, W. B. 1963. "The Economics of Newspapers." *Economic Journal* 73:201–18.

Reed, T. H. 1937. "Commercial Broadcasting and Civic Education." *Public Opinion Quarterly* 1:57–67.

Reynolds, G. 2006. *An Army of Davids: How Markets and Technology Empower Ordinary People to Beat Big Media, Big Government, and Other Goliaths*. Washington, DC: Nelson Current.

Reynolds, G., and H. Reynolds. 2006. "The Glenn and Helen Show: Interviewing Chris Anderson about the Long Tail." Blog post with link to podcast, July 11. http://instapundit.com/archives/031380.php.

Rheingold, H. 2003. *Smart Mobs: The Next Social Revolution*. New York: Basic Books.

Rogers, R. 2004. *Information Politics on the Web*. Cambridge, MA: MIT Press.

Roscoe, T. 1999. "The Construction of the World Wide Web Audience." *Media, Culture, and Society* 21:673–84.

Rosen, J. 2004. "Your Blog or Mine?" *New York Times Magazine*, December 19, 24.

Rosenstone, S. J., and M. Hansen. 1993. *Mobilization, Participation, and Democracy in America.* New York: Macmillan.

Rosse, J. N. 1967. "Daily Newspapers, Monopolistic Competition, and Economies of Scale." *American Economic Review* 57:522–33.

———. 1970. "Estimating Cost Function Parameters without Using Cost Data: Illustrated Methodology." *Econometrica* 38:256–75.

———. 1980. "The Decline of Direct Newspaper Competition." *Journal of Competition* 30:65–71.

Rothenberg, R. 2007. "An Open Letter to comScore and Nielsen//NetRatings." Interactive Adversting Bureau, New York: April 20. http://www.iab.net /news/pr_2007_04_20.asp.

Saad, L. 2005. *Blogs Not Yet in the Media Big Leagues.* Report, March 11. Princeton, NJ: Gallup.

Samuelson, R. J. 2004. "Bull Market for Media Bias." *Washington Post*, June 23, A21.

Sanders, L. M. 1997. "Against Deliberation." *Political Theory* 25:347–76.

Schattschneider, E. E. 1960. *The Semisovereign People: A Realist's View of Democracy in America.* New York: Holt, Rinchart and Winston.

Schudson, M. 1999. *The Good Citizen: A History of American Civic Life.* Cambridge, MA: Harvard University Press.

Scott, E. 2004. " 'Big Media' Meets the 'Blogger': Coverage of Trent Lott's Remarks at Strom Thurmond's Birthday Party." Kennedy School of Government Case Program. Case 1731, March. http://www.ksg.harvard .edu/presspol/Research_Publications/Case_Studies/1731_0.pdf.

Seipp, C. 2002. "Online Uprising." *American Journalism Review*, June, 42.

Semel, T. 2006. "Navigating Yahoo!" Interview with Ken Auletta, May 11. http://www.newyorker.com/videos/060511onvi_video_semel.

Seper, C. 2004a. "Can Blogs Claim Victory in Blocking Anti-Kerry Film?" *Cleveland Plain Dealer*, October 21, A18.

———. 2004b. "For Good or Ill, Blogs Make Waves." *Cleveland Plain Dealer*, October 7, A1.

Shafer, J. 2006. "Judith Miller's New Excuse." Slate, March 16. http://www .slate.com/id/2138161/.

Shah, D. V., N. Kwak, and R. L. Holbert. 2001. " 'Connecting' and 'Disconnecting' with Civic Life: Patterns of Internet Use and the Production of Social Capital." *Political Communication* 18:141–62.

Shah, D. V., J. M. McLeod, and S. H. Yoon. 2001. "Communication, Context, and Community: An Exploration of Print, Broadcast, and Internet Influences." *Communication Research* 28:464–506.

Shapiro, A. L. 1999 *The Control Revolution*. New York: Public Affairs.

Shirky, C. 2004. "Inequality in the Weblog World." Seminar presentation at the Berkman Center for Internet and Society, Harvard Law School, January 24.

Silverstein, C., M. Henzinger, H. Marais, and M. Moricz. 1998. "Analysis of a Very Large AltaVista Query Log." *SRC Technical Note* 1998-014, October 26.

Smith, J. 2001. "Globalizing Resistance: The Battle of Seattle and the Future of Social Movements." *Mobilization: An International Quarterly* 6:1–19.

Smolkin, R. 2004. "Photos of the Fallen." *American Journalism Review* (June–July): 38.

Snider, J. H. 1996. "New Media, Potential Information, and Democratic Accountability: A Case Study of Governmental Access Community Media." Paper presented at the annual meeting of the American Political Science Association, San Francisco, 1996, August 28–September 1.

———. 2001. "E-Democracy as Deterrence: Public Policy Implications of a Deterrence Model of Democratic Accountability." Paper presented at the annual meeting of the American Political Science Association, San Francisco, August 30–September 2.

Snider, P. B. 1967. "Mr. Gates Revisited: A 1966 Version of the 1949 Case Study." *Journalism Quarterly* 44:419–27.

Song, C., S. Havlin, and H. A. Makse. 2005. "Self-Similarity of Complex Networks." *Nature* 433:392–95.

Soto, M. 2001. "New Toys R Us Venture a Novel Strategy for Amazon.com." *Seattle Times*, May 23, D1.

Spink, A., S. Ozmutlu, H. C. Ozmutlu, and B. J. Jansen. 2002. "U.S. versus European Web Searching Trends." *ACM SIGIR Forum* 36:32–38.

Starr, P. 2004. *The Creation of the American Media: The Political Origins of Modern Communications*. New York: Basic Books.

Stone, L. 2004. "A Nod to Blogs: More Views for the Grass Roots to Graze On." *Los Angeles Times*, July 30, E35.

Stromer-Galley, J. 2000. "On-line Interaction and Why Candidates Avoid It." *Journal of Communication* 50:111–32.

Sundar, S. S., S. Kalyanaraman, and J. Brown. 2003. "Explicating Web Site Interactivity." *Communication Research* 30:30–59.

Sunstein, C. 2001. *Republic.com*. Princeton, NJ: Princeton University Press.

———. 2006. *Infoopia*. New York: Oxford University Press.

Tancer, B. 2006. "Google Breaks 60 Percent: U.S. July Search Volume Numbers." Hitwise Competitive Intelligence, blog post, August 3. http://weblogs.hitwise.com/bill-tancer/2006/08/us_july_search_volume_numbers.html.

Taube, M. 2004. "Bravo to the Bloggers Who Felled a Network." *Toronto Star*, September 22, 19.

Thierer, A., and C. W. Crews. 2003. "Google as Public Utility? No Results in This Search for Monopoly." *IT and T News*, December 1. http://www .heartland.org/Article.cfm?artId=13765.

Tolbert, C. J., and R. S. McNeal. 2003. "Unraveling the Effects of the Internet on Political Participation?" *Political Research Quarterly* 56:175–85.

Tomlin, J. A. 2003. "A New Paradigm for Ranking Pages on the World Wide Web." In *Proceedings of the Twelfth International World Wide Web Conference*, 350–55. New York: ACM Press.

Trippi, J. 2005. *The Revolution Will Not Be Televised: Democracy, the Internet, and the Overthrow of Everything.* New York: Regan Books.

U.S. Census Bureau. 2001. "Households and Families." Census 2000 brief, Washington, DC, September. http://www.census.gov/prod/2001pubs/ c2kbr01-8.pdf.

Verba S., K. L. Schlozman, and H. E. Brady. 1995. *Voice and Equality.* Cambridge, MA: Harvard University Press.

von Sternberg, B. 2004. "From Geek to Chic: Blogs Gain Influence." *Minneapolis Star-Tribune*, September 22, 1A.

Wallsten, P. 2004a. " 'Buckhead,' Who Said CBS Memos Were Forged, Is a GOP-Linked Attorney." *Seattle Times*, September 18. http://seattletimes .nwsource.com/html/nationworld/2002039080_buckhead18.html.

———. 2004b. "No Disputing It: Blogs Are Major Players." *New York Times*, September 12, A22.

Ward, S., P. Nixon, and R. Gibson. 2003. "Political Parties and the Internet: An Overview." In *Net Gain? Political Parties and the Internet*, ed. R. Gibson, P. Nixon, and S. Ward, 11–39. London: Routledge.

Warschauer, M. 2004. *Technology and Social Inclusion: Rethinking the Digital Divide.* Cambridge, MA: MIT Press.

Wayne, L., and J. Zeleny. 2008. "Enlisting New Donors, Obama Reaped $32 Million in January." *New York Times*, February. http://www.nytimes.com/ 2008/02/01/us/politics/01donate.html.

"Web of Politics." 2004. *San Francisco Chronicle*, October 25, B6.

Weiss, J. 2003. "Blogs Shake the Political Discourse: Website Bloggers Changing the Face of Political Campaigns." *Boston Globe*, July 23, A1.

White, D. M. 1950. "The 'Gatekeeper': A Case Study in the Selection of News." *Journalism Quarterly* 27:383–90.

Whittington, L. 2005. "Byrd Raises $1.2 for Next Year's Election." *Roll Call*, April 14.

Wilhelm, A. G. 2000. *Democracy in the Digital Age: Challenges to Political Life in Cyberspace.* London: Routledge.

Williams, A. 2004. "Blogged in Boston: Politics Gets an Unruly Spin." *New York Times*, August 1, sec. 9, 1.

Williams, B. A., and M. X. Delli Carpini. 2000. "Unchained Reaction: The Collapse of Media Gatekeeping and the Clinton-Lewinsky Scandal." *Journalism* 1:61–85.

Williams, C., B. Weinberg, and J. Gordon. 2004. "When Online and Offline Politics 'Meetup.' " Paper presented at the annual American Political Science Association conference, Chicago, September 2–5. http://meetupsurvey.com/study/components/reports/APSApaperfinal.doc.

Wood, D. B. 2004. "At the DNC, It's a Blog-Eat-Blog World." *Christian Science Monitor*, July 27, 10.

Yahoo!, Inc. 2005. *Annual Report*. http://edgar.sec.gov.

Yeager, H. 2004. "Blogs, Bias, and 24-Hour News." *Financial Times*, September 24, 17

Yim, J. 2003. "Audience Concentration in the Media: Cross-Media Comparisons and the Introduction of the Uncertainty Measure. *Communication Monographs* 70:114–28.

Zaller, J. 1992. *The Nature and Origins of Mass Opinion*. Cambridge: Cambridge University Press.

———. 2003. "A New Standard of News Quality: Burglar Alarms for the Monitorial Citizen." *Political Communication* 20:109–30.

Zeleny, J., and K. Seelye. 2008. "More Money Is Pouring In for Clinton and Obama." *New York Times*, March 7. http://www.nytimes.com/2008/03/07/us/politics/07campaign.html.

Index